Car Finance - A Simple Guide

An Amazing Motoring Guide From Graham Hill, The World's Number One Car Finance Blogger

Graham Hill

DISCLAIMER

©Copyright Graham Hill 2011

All rights reserved. No part of this publication to be reproduced, copied or transmitted by any means (graphic, electronic or mechanical, including photocopying, recording, taping, or information and retrieval systems) without written permission of the copyright holder.

Any person who does any unauthorised act in relation to this publication may be liable to criminal prosecution and civil claims for damages.

This publication is intended to provide accurate information in regard to the subject-matter covered. Readers entering into transactions on the basis of such information should seek the services of a competent professional advisor, as the publication is made available on the understanding that neither the publisher nor the author is engaged in rendering legal or accounting advice or other professional services. The publisher, author and editor expressly disclaim all and any liability and responsibility to any person, whether a purchaser or reader of this publication or not, in respect of anything, and of the consequences of anything, done or omitted to be done by any such person in reliance, whether wholly or partially, upon the whole or any part of the contents of this publication.

For details of training available to those providing vehicle finance information to consumers, businesses or staff, please contact Graham Hill at the email address shown below:

Published by:

GHAF Publishing

email address: ghaf@ghafinance.co.uk

Join my blog:
http://www.thebestcarfinanceblog.co.uk

1st Edition December 2011

ISBN-13: 978-1475225792
ISBN-10: 1475225792

Table of Contents

About Graham Hill 1

Guide To Car Finance 3

Introduction 5

The Credit Crunch 7

Section 1: Preparing For Credit 9

    Late Credit Card Payments: 10

    County Court Judgements 11

    Arrears & Defaults 13

    Electoral Roll 15

    Financial Links To Others With Poor Credit ... 17

    Bank Account 19

    Employment 21

    Guarantor 22

    Credit Union 23

    Summary 24

Section 2: Funding Methods 31

Personal Loan – Secured 32

Unsecured Personal Loan 35

Hire Purchase 39

Personal Contract Purchase (PCP) 46

Contract Hire & Personal Contract Hire (PCH) 51

Personal Contract Hire 66

Section 3: What To Do When Things Go Wrong Part 1 69

General Advice 69

Prioritise Your Debt 79

Your Broker 80

Making Contact 80

Mortgage Rescue Scheme 82

30 Day Rule 83

Debt Relief Order/Bankruptcy 84

Guarantees/Indemnities 85

What To Do When Things Go Wrong Part 2 89

- Personal Loan - Secured 89
- Personal Loan - Unsecured.. 91
- Hire Purchase/Personal Contract Purchase (PCP) 96
- Contract Hire & Personal Contract Hire (PCH) 100
- Notice Of Correction 104

Conclusion 107

Addendum: The Effects Of The EU Consumer Credit Act 109

- Who's Affected? 111
- Key Changes 111
- Early Repayment 111
- Contractual Information 112
- APR Calculation 113
- Variation of Interest Rates 113
- Credit Intermediaries 114
- Exemptions 114
- New Requirements 115

Adequate Explanations	115
Requirement to Assess Credit Worthiness	117
Requirement Concerning Credit Reference Databases	117
Right of Withdrawal	118
Voluntary Termination	119
Assignment of Rights	120
'Out of Scope' Agreements	120
Business Lending	121
Loans Above £60,260	122
Advertisements	123
Conclusion	125
Contacts & Resources	127

About Graham Hill

Graham Hill is regarded as the UK's leading vehicle finance expert. He is also the world's number 1 car finance blogger, as can be found on Google, when you search Car Finance Blog, number 1 out of around 200 million.

Graham writes a regular column in the prestige Motor Finance journal under the name of The Arranger. He has also written several articles in National newspapers and magazines and has appeared on BBC Radio 4's award winning Money Box Program. He has been chairman of the British Lease Brokers Association and President of the National Association of Commercial Finance Brokers.

Graham, an accountant, has helped thousands of clients to save fortunes whilst driving cars that were better than they ever thought possible. He has been a consultant to several finance companies including Yes Car Credit and advised online used car seller carsite.co.uk

To keep up to date with car finance and motor industry changes visit www.thebestcarfinanceblog.co.uk and sign up to the blog, there's a free gift waiting for you there. You can also make contact with Graham if you are experiencing problems and need some help.

Note From Graham Hill:

I hope that you find this book interesting and by following my advice you manage to reduce your motoring costs substantially whilst, at the same time, driving a great car. Please visit my blog and keep up to date with the latest information regarding the various finance methods, how to find the best deals and any scams that are being perpetrated that you need to avoid. Happy motoring.

Graham Hill

Guide To Car Finance

This guide has been specifically compiled for both small businesses and consumers by Graham Hill, considered by many to be the UK's foremost authority on the subject of Motor Finance. Graham has been in the industry for over 25 years starting life as an accountant then specialising in Car Finance at a time when there were very few legal controls and not too many options. Graham points out 'In my next book I list over 40 genuine ways to finance your car. So selecting just one is a potential minefield when considering the best option for your individual needs.'

Graham has previously written a book entitled An Insider Guide To Car Finance, he has been a consultant to several finance providers as already stated and writes prolifically for various journals and newspapers as well as his number 1 blog. He also plays an active part in various steering committees and debating groups including regular attendance at meetings held at the University of Buckingham.

Introduction

In this guide I'm going to provide you with guidance that will assist you in arranging credit, then help you to decide upon the best finance option that matches your circumstances and finally what to do when things go wrong. I will also explain why some finance, which might look great to begin with, may end up costing you your possessions, and possibly your home, even when the finance isn't secured against it.

During the credit crunch it is vitally important that you '**Put Finance First**'. There is no point in test driving cars and getting excited if you are not going to be able to arrange finance or the finance is going to be far too expensive. So, make sure that you don't have any nasties appearing on your credit file that would put off a lender and don't assume anything. People who have had no problems for years and believe that they have a perfect credit rating are being declined for car finance. The situation is catching out many applicants. I'll explain more of this later.

Once I've provided you with the best chance of arranging finance, I'm briefly going to cover some of the more popular ways to finance a car along with their relative advantages and disadvantages.

Finally, what can you do if the unexpected happens, i.e. you lose your job, you are sick, you lose a loved one, what can you do to mitigate the problem? I'll give you some advice that may not only help to resolve the problem but also protect your precious credit rating.

For a more detailed insight into all the options available along with tons of advice you can keep up to date by visiting my blog:

http://thebestcarfinanceblog.co.uk.

The Credit Crunch

Go back to the middle of 2007 and around 60% of all applicants for car finance were approved on what is known as prime rate, i.e. the lowest rate. Currently we are down to around 40% and some lenders are down to between 20% and 25%. So this section is vitally important if you are to be offered finance at the best possible rate.

First of all, what is a credit crunch? Very simply, it is a lack of money available to lend. For a lender, that is part of a banking group, to be able to provide you with money with which to finance your car, he relies on the money he and the bank have loaned to borrowers being repaid and savers depositing money that he can then lend out. The problem is, therefore, twofold: as a result of the recession more borrowers are slipping into arrears, or defaulting on their payments altogether, and savers are investing money wherever they can achieve the best interest rates, and that is certainly not the banks, starving the banks and other similar lenders of cash to lend. In addition, the banks have been forced to strengthen their balance sheets by building up reserves and therefore lend less. The result, what is known as a credit crunch.

With less money available lenders are, therefore, only taking the cream of applicants. This means that even a few late credit card payments or a missed mortgage payment, something that may have been overlooked before, could result in you being declined for credit. As I point out in my book, 'An Insider Guide To Car Finance' even your postcode or marital status can make the difference between receiving credit and being declined, so giving yourself the best opportunity, by preparing yourself for credit, is vitally important. And the best time to prepare is when you don't need it. So even if you don't intend changing your car within the next 12 months you would be wise to take action now.

Section 1: Preparing For Credit

So with less money to lend, resulting in fewer applicants being approved for finance, is there anything you can do to help your application? Yes there is. First of all you need to get an up-to-date copy of your credit report to see if it contains any nasties that need to be addressed. You can send a letter into any of the credit reference agencies along with a £2 fee and they will send back a copy of your report. Or you can obtain a copy for free by visiting the website of Equifax, or any other credit reference agency. You have to provide your credit card details and they will charge your card monthly, which will give you access to your credit report at any time you want or you can download your current report then cancel the arrangement, but I think it's useful to check your credit report every month. They will also issue email alerts if there is any activity on your account, so if a new credit card is opened or a loan taken out you will be advised which could help to prevent credit fraud and cloning of your details in the future.

Once you have your credit report you need to check it carefully to see if there is anything adverse registered or anything that looks particularly bad, then decide if it is accurate or not. It may help to consider the following:

Late Credit Card Payments:

This will be shown by numbers in the history details, representing how far behind you have slipped into arrears. If you see a 1 it means you were one payment late, 2 = 2 payments late, 3 = 3 payments late, etc. A few number 1's are normally ignored but if you often forget to pay and end up paying a few days late each time, causing several 1's to appear, this will affect your credit rating. In addition late payments normally attract a cost of £12 from the credit card company each time it happens. So the first thing you should do is arrange for all of your cards to be paid, as minimum payment, by direct debit. You can always pay more off if you wish by debit card, at your bank or online. That will certainly clean up your credit card payments and will help to improve your credit score.

On a positive note having a credit card can be very useful when it comes to increasing your credit score and preparing for finance. My advice would be to take out a credit card and use it say once a month, showing some activity. Do a little bit of shopping or fill up the car with fuel using the card. Then pay off all but a very small balance of say £5 so that interest charges will be applied to the account. This will be just pennies but having a credit card with regular use may just give you the few extra points that achieve an acceptance on a car at the lowest rate that could save you hundreds of pounds. A credit card can be useful for other purposes so I strongly recommend that you apply for one. More about this later.

In truth, obtaining a credit card is one of the easiest ways to recover your credit as there are credit cards such as Vanquish and Capital One that are aimed at those with poor credit. The rates are extremely high at around 30% APR so you don't want to keep a balance on your account of more than £5. But constant use and payment of the card will help to increase your credit score. If you are declined for one of these high interest rate cards you can still get yourself a pre-paid credit card. This card enables you to pay money into your account then spend this money using your credit card as you would any other credit card. This isn't quite as good as having a true credit card but every little helps.

County Court Judgements

If you have a dispute, with someone you owe money to, always try to resolve the matter with them directly. If you can't afford to pay all of the debt in one go, arrange to pay it over a period in order to avoid going to court, that way you avoid a county court judgement (CCJ) which can have a major negative effect on your credit rating. Even if the CCJ doesn't relate to a credit transaction.

Section 1: Preparing For Credit

If you end up in court and lose the case you will be ordered to pay within a set period, normally one month. If you pay within this period the CCJ will not be listed on the Register of Judgements, Orders and Fines, which is the source used by the credit reference agencies for listing CCJ details on your credit file. If you cannot pay the judgement immediately but you don't need to spread the costs you can make full payment direct to the person/company that you owe the money to – but make sure that you ask for a receipt for the money sent. You then need to contact the court in order to have the CCJ removed (if paid within the month) or marked as 'satisfied' if paid in full later.

You can request from the court time to pay: if this is allowed you will agree a monthly payment and period with the judge. The CCJ will then remain as unpaid until you have fully paid it when you can request that it is marked 'satisfied'. Whether you pay the CCJ in full or spread over a period, you still need to obtain a receipt from the other party. If you are not given a receipt from the person you paid and he has not advised the court that you have paid in full, the court will write to him to confirm receipt of money. Once they receive notice that this amount has been paid, from the other party, they will mark the CCJ as satisfied.

Interestingly, if the court doesn't hear from the other party within a month of sending the letter, requesting confirmation of payment, they will either remove the CCJ (within a month of issue of the CCJ) or mark it as satisfied. So it may be possible that if a company has subsequently gone bankrupt and therefore does not answer a letter from the court, a CCJ could be marked as 'satisfied' even though it hasn't been paid. I would recommend taking legal advice if you find yourself in this situation. Don't forget, if you end up with a CCJ it will stay on the register for 6 years, even if it is satisfied. But careful management of your credit file could certainly improve your credit rating.

It is important to make sure that your credit file is accurate and up to date. If you have had a CCJ issued against you and you have paid it in full make sure that this is shown on the credit file. If there are special circumstances relating to the CCJ you can post a Notice of Correction on your credit file to bring the special circumstances to the notice of the lender – more of this later.

Arrears & Defaults

Arrears are bad but defaults are a complete no no! It is very unlikely that you will be offered prime (low rate) finance if you have a default registered against a credit arrangement such as a loan or HP. First of all you must check your credit file and see if there are any arrears or defaults that need to be addressed.

Section 1: Preparing For Credit

Before you get to this stage, one of the most important things to do, if you get into trouble, is call the person you owe money to – I'll talk more about this later.

If you have arrears on your credit file, i.e. you have missed payments on a credit arrangement, it stays on your credit file for up to 36 months. So, if it is incorrect, you must tell the credit reference agencies immediately and the person/company that has registered the arrears. Defaults will stay on your credit files for 6 years, so it is even more important that you take action as soon as possible. If you have a default that is incorrect you must do the same as you would with arrears in order to have it removed. You will need to complete a Notice of Dispute which can be done online by visiting each of the credit reference agency websites and completing the online form.

If any information held on your credit file is incorrect then you have rights under the Data Protection Act 1998 to have the information removed. Contact the credit reference agencies by phone or post in order to obtain the procedures in the event that you are unable to do it online. In the meantime use a Notice Of Correction (see below) to put an explanation on your credit files.

If there is a reason why you had problems that caused the arrears or defaults, e.g. illness, redundancy etc., then you can use a Notice of Correction (see below) to tell lenders all about it. Although lenders don't always agree with me, I think someone who has had problems and manages to bring their credit back in order, they are a better risk than someone who has never had a problem. More about this later.

It is important that you communicate with lenders as soon as possible if you find yourself in trouble. Always try to come to an arrangement with the lender before you fall into arrears or default and always try to avoid going to court and being issued with a CCJ. The court may well end up making an order to pay exactly the same as you would have paid if you had negotiated with the lender in the first place but if the arrangement had been agreed with the lender you would have had no CCJ appearing on your credit file. I'll talk more about this in the final section but the time to prepare for finance is when you don't need it and make sure that you deal with problems before they get out of hand.

Electoral Roll

Lenders see this as key to providing you with credit, as all credit information is linked to your home address, and, if you are not shown where you say you live and have lived there as long as you say you have lived there, the lender becomes very nervous and could decline your application.

It is very important that you can be found at your current address, so make sure that you are on the electoral register. By not registering the lender may assume that you are trying to avoid paying your council tax so you may try to avoid repaying any finance. Since 16th January 2001 you have been able to register at any time of the year so, if your credit file search shows that you are not on the Electoral Roll, you should apply immediately and make sure you return the form to your local council every September.

If you don't show up at previous addresses prepare to be asked for proofs of your old addresses, so dig out old bank statements, credit card statements, utility bills etc. to prove that you lived there and, of course, it is useful to hold on to a few old bills when you move house – just in case.

I have had some applicants in the past who have said that they don't agree with the voting system in this country so would never vote and therefore have never completed the form used to place them on the Electoral Register. Whilst they are, of course, free to hold these views, it doesn't help when applying for credit. If the lender uses credit scoring you could easily drop enough points to be refused credit, so make sure that you are on the register even if you have no intention of voting.

If a gap appears for genuine reasons, you can again use the Notice of Correction to advise any lender of the special circumstances. For example, you may have lived abroad for a period as part of a long holiday or as part of your job. Or you may have moved in with a sick relative and rented your house out to someone whilst you were away. This information would be of help to the lender, so make sure he receives it by posting it on the credit files – all of them.

Financial Links To Others With Poor Credit

Years ago credit searches were carried out by household, so if a search was carried out on you it would reveal the credit history of all occupants of the property, which could often lead to a finance application being declined as a result of others living at the same property, even if they were not related or had any association with the applicant. Typically, where a house was converted to several flats, one of the tenants who had a poor credit status could cause all others to be declined for finance.

Also, parents could be declined for credit, quite unfairly, as a result of children who were living at home having a poor credit history. This has now changed and when a search is carried out it can only be taken out on the person who is applying for credit. However, there are two exceptions. Firstly, if you agree that searches can be carried out on others that you live with and they also agree.

This can be helpful if a child or partner has never had credit before and the credit status of the other person could assist their application, often without the need for a joint application or guarantee. The other exception is where a joint financial arrangement has been entered into by you and either one or several others living at the same address. The company carrying out the search can search all files and would consider seriously any poor credit that the other party or parties have recorded against them.

A joint financial arrangement could be a mortgage, credit cards or even joint names on the supply of a utility or mobile phone. But the situation is much worse than this, **you don't actually have to be in a joint arrangement**, you simply have to make an application. So if you have applied for a credit card, for example, in two names, this is considered a joint financial arrangement, even if you don't take the card the record remains unless you formally request to have the joint arrangement removed from your credit file on the basis that you entered into no such agreement.

So, it is important that you check your credit file for any joint arrangements being recorded, as this could hamper your application. If you have a financial link to others which may be detrimental, you should contact the credit reference agents and request that they remove the link, unless of course it is unavoidable as you already have joint loans, mortgages or credit cards. You can request that the link be removed by completing a Notice of Disassociation online.

Bank Account

Most lenders will want to take their monthly payments by direct debit, so it is essential that you have a bank or building society account that is capable of accepting direct debits. It is, therefore, important to make sure that you have opened a bank account before making a finance application. It is not so difficult these days, even with poor credit, to arrange for a bank account but expect to have some tough controls imposed if your credit file shows some adverse (bad) information.

To start with you should be able to open a basic current account with just a debit card or cash card. Opening an account with a deposit is always good so, even though the money may not stay in your account for long, it will gain favour with the bank manager. If you have problems, it may be worth opening a savings account with a building society, who will normally allow you to open a current account after 6 months of regular savings. Check with the building society first.

You won't be able to use the savings account to pay the direct debits. If you haven't got a bank account you may be able to take out a finance agreement in joint names with someone else, such as family, friends or a partner who has an account, but due to the liability implications, i.e. you are both liable for the debt, this is not a route I would recommend.

Whilst on the subject of bank accounts, some people think that when you are asked for copies of your bank statements by the lender that they are checking to see if you are overdrawn. This can be a factor but if the lender sees that you have an overdraft facility of £1,000 but you never go over £200 overdrawn this can look good, especially as your bank, who knows you best of all, is prepared to allow an overdraft.

The real no no, and the thing that would cause you to be declined for finance, is one or more instances of returned items, i.e. where the bank would not honour a direct debit or cheque that you have raised to pay a bill. If there is something like this on your account, which may not have been your fault, you should wait to make an application until you have three complete months during which no payments have been returned. Finance companies normally only request 3 months bank statements when they ask, hence the reason for me mentioning 3 months.

As an extra piece of advice – if you know that you are going to have a problem meeting your direct debits, cancel them immediately, then re-set them up. Firstly, you won't incur bank charges for 'bouncing' the payment and nothing will appear on your bank statement to show that you have a returned item. However, if you can't make the payment immediately, beware of an arrears note being posted to your credit file.

Employment

In order to qualify for most finance, and certainly the finance that attracts the lowest interest rate, you need to have an income. There are no hard and fast rules about employment but generally you won't qualify if you are simply on benefits, unless you are disabled, then you may qualify for the Government Motobility Scheme.

You may still be able to arrange finance without being employed if you have some proof of income showing that you can make the finance repayments. This could be a pension, annuity, benefactor payments, divorce settlement or rental income, as long as it can be proven. For most applicants you will need to be able to prove that you have a job and that you have regular income. To show what can be done I arranged a lease for an 83 year old gentleman receiving just pensions in 2011. Age isn't a problem as long as you have proof of income.

We used to specify that you had to have a full time job before you could be considered for finance but with some people able to earn as much in part time employment as others in full time – it is simply down to your ability to make your repayments

Guarantor

When preparing for finance if your credit score is low (your credit report gives guidance here) you might like to consider discussing with family or friends to see if any would act as a guarantor. This can be quite dangerous for both parties but could be a lifeline if you can't obtain credit in your own right whilst potentially achieving a lower APR. Having a guarantor can put more pressure on you as any failure on your part passes responsibility for payment to your guarantor. If you act as a guarantor nothing appears on your credit file so your credit score isn't affected. Provided the contractual payments are made on time your guarantor will remain unaffected.

However, if you miss payments the lender will attempt to recover the money owed from your guarantor. If he also fails to make the payments then the default will be registered on the guarantor's credit file, as well as yours, which will affect his credit, in the future, as well as yours. Another alternative would be to apply for finance in joint names. When you do this both parties are jointly and severally liable for the payments. This means that the loan is registered against both parties to the contract with any arrears or defaults registered against both. However, whilst some lenders won't accept a guarantor they may accept joint applicants. Again this could be useful if you have a poor credit score but as this is a linked transaction, if your partner in the agreement has strong credit this may be weakened if a lender is searching your partner and finds a link from him to you with poor credit.

Credit Union

I'm not going to cover Credit Union in depth here, I do that in my next book, but in preparing for credit it is wise to open a Credit Union account if you have access to one. Providing you have been regularly saving small amounts you will be able to take out a loan with the Union. They rely more on their knowledge of you rather than your credit score. In the past Credit Unions have not registered your loan with the credit reference agencies so whilst you may be a good payer it doesn't get registered. However, at the time of writing, the situation was changing and some Credit Unions were starting to record their loans with at least one of the credit reference agencies. This is great news as it is easier to obtain a loan through a Credit Union and by recording a good payment history this will help you to obtain low rate loans in the future. All good preparation.

Summary

To summarize – you need to prepare for finance long before you need to apply. If you can, put as many of your debts on direct debit payments because even late credit card payments will potentially cause you to have a loan application refused.

Check your credit report and, if you find an error, apply to have it repaired, but also file a notice of correction, which is free, but make sure you file it with all three credit reference agencies. If you have filed a notice of correction, the file MUST be looked at by an underwriter, they cannot simply auto approve or decline an application based on credit score – so this information is of vital importance. Follow the Notice Of Correction Rules, be concise as you are limited to the number of words you can use. Also, don't make personal comments or be insulting when referring to an ex who left you with a debt or anyone else you may hold responsible. Finance companies and mobile phone providers may upset you but all the underwriter wants to see are the facts – as you see them.

Not all intermediaries such as car dealers, brokers and bank staff are of equal knowledge when it comes to finance. Not all share my accountancy background and 25 years as a broker, consultant, commentator and top blogger so you may have to help yourself by making sure that you provide as much information as possible with your application. Don't lie on your application or provide false proofs of identity or address.

If you are found to have acted fraudulently you may be reported to the police or reported on the Credit Industry Fraud Avoidance Service (CIFAS) register. So even though there may not be sufficient evidence to prosecute, you may still appear on the register as a warning to other lenders.

Some may disagree with me giving this next piece of advice, especially as you won't see it anywhere else. But everything needs close attention if your finance application is to be successful. When a lender offers low lease rates or low APR's it follows that he will only want to provide these low profit rates to those with the lowest risk or highest credit score. This means that as few as 20% could succeed in achieving the very best rates so every detail of your finance application is important.

This brings me to your bank and credit card statements. You should plan well in advance for your finance application. With regard to your credit cards, if you feel that you may not be able to make your minimum payment next month but you are making more than the minimum payment this month you should keep some money back in order to make your minimum payment next month. I've even taken money from one card in order pay another card on time as a result of one of my customers paying me late. I don't recommend this as a permanent arrangement but it's legal to do so and it helps to keep your credit score high. When applying for finance it's important that no arrears appear on your credit report.

This brings me to your bank account. Definitely don't have any returned items appearing on your bank statements during the 3 months prior to your finance application. If you have a problem and can't make a direct debit payment, cancel your direct debit, pay by cheque or debit card, then reinstate the direct debit. That way no adverse is shown on your credit file as you've avoided a returned item. If you are constantly in overdraft it may help if you can put some money into your account to take you back into the black, even if only for a short period. The couple of extra points could make all the difference.

Having many searches on your credit file could also affect your ability to obtain credit. If you search your own file it doesn't register as a search on the credit file but each time a lender searches your file it is registered. If you collect more than 3 searches within a short space of time it will cause lenders to take a closer look at your application. For some it will result in an auto decline.

If you use an online broker advertising low rates he could be making as little as £100 on your deal so don't expect any exceptional customer support. In order to save time it has been known that some will submit your finance application to several lenders at the same time so that even if you are declined by one, often the cheapest as they are looking for perfect credit, you may be accepted by another so that the broker can offer you an acceptance at a higher rate. If you refuse you may find additional problems when you go elsewhere as a result of the number of times your credit file has been searched. It's known as the scatter gun approach. My advice here is don't simply go for the cheapest, know the broker you are dealing with and if possible only use brokers to whom you are referred.

In preparation make sure you have two utility bills dated within the last 3 months or credit card statements/bank statements, all showing your current address as proof of address. If you are asked for a bank statement as proof of address don't send one with any adverse entries on it. Better still blank out the transactions if the lender has only asked for one page as proof of address. I had a client approved for credit but was asked for a bank statement showing his address. When he sent it across to the lender they withdrew the offer of finance as he had several returned items on the statement. Had he not shown the transactions he would have been fine. Only provide what you are asked for.

Make sure that the address on your driving licence is up to date, lenders have declined finance in the past for not having a driving licence with a current address on it. You could also be fined up to £1,000 for having a licence showing an out of date address so it makes sense to get it altered.

Finally, if you find on your credit file that you have linked financial transactions with someone with poor credit, try to have the links removed. If it was simply a search, then you can request to have the link removed by contacting the credit reference agencies. If you have a joint loan, mortgage or credit card, see if you can move everything into one name, preferably the other person if there had been any late payments or defaults. You need to present a case that's whiter than white in the current economic climate. Use a Notice Of Disassociation to remove links between you and whoever you may have finance links to who has an adverse credit history.

When applying as a business make sure that you also prepare beforehand. It is not wise to apply for finance if a director has poor credit. I've known of directors asked to resign as a director to facilitate a finance application. Also partners have resigned from a partnership for the same reason. If directors or partners won't resign it is wise, when completing an application form, to list the weakest, in terms of credit, at the end of the application as some lenders only search the first two on the list. And if you are only asked for two partners or directors, just provide details of two particularly if others have questionable credit.

For continual updates, advice and information please sign into my world leading blog and receive copies of my regular newsletter:

http://www.thebestcarfinanceblog.co.uk

Section 2: Funding Methods

In this section I will cover some of the most popular ways to finance your car. In fact I have identified over 40 ways to finance a car. I have put all of these methods into my next book which will be available soon – keep an eye on my blog.

When it comes to new cars, dealer HP is still the most popular way to finance a car. That is according to the Finance and Leasing Association (FLA). However, it is far more difficult to identify the finance methods used for funding used cars. Personal loans are not always identified as being used to finance a car, with the same problem of identification applied to extensions/increases to mortgages and cash payments.

In my opinion, personal loans account for most car finance, followed by HP, then Personal Contract Purchase followed, finally, by the method that is gaining ground – Contract Hire, already popular with business users but becoming more widely accepted amongst personal users as Personal Contract Hire (PCH). I will be explaining these methods along with personal loans split between secured personal loans and unsecured personal loans - the only finance that can be used to finance private car purchases.

Personal Loan – Secured

These types of loan are offered by banks, building societies and specialist lenders. Whilst most secured loans are secured against your home you can, in theory, offer up any property that you own, provided it is acceptable to the lender, but bear in mind that if you default you could lose the property on which the loan was secured. You may be able to borrow against tangible things including jewelry, paintings, collections (such as stamp or coin collections) and land, or intangibles including a pension fund, endowment, investments (stocks and shares) etc, although they must have a value in excess of the money you wish to borrow. This is known as loan to value (of the goods against which the loan is secured). Generally, the higher the loan to value, the higher the risk and the higher the interest rate.

People normally consider a secured loan for amounts over £25,000. It is also usual to spread the cost over a longer period than an unsecured loan, although I don't recommend that you use this method for financing a car that you may only keep for 2 or 3 years.

Most people use their home as security, which would require the lender to take a charge on the property. The charge for the secured loan is normally a second charge, with the first charge being your mortgage.

A charge means that, if the house is sold, the holder of the charge is paid from the proceeds of sale. This is quite good from a borrower's point of view because, if you are still paying your mortgage, it is unlikely that the mortgage company or the courts would allow a repossession to go through, certainly not in the current climate, so the lender would have to wait until you sold your house to recover his money.

But you should be warned that it could happen, hence the warning that the lenders must all give you 'your home may be at risk if you don't keep up payments secured against it'. If you have not made every effort to make repayments or at least pay something, the second charge holder could go to court to force you to sell your house and, if the judge isn't in a good mood or feels you haven't done everything you could have done, he could grant a repossession order.

When taking out a secured loan, you may be tempted to take the loan over a long period but intend to pay the loan off when you can afford to, in which case check the early settlement penalties, they vary from lender to lender. If you intend to settle early it may be worth paying a slightly higher interest rate in order to avoid high early settlement costs.

You will normally find that the interest charged on a secured loan is higher than a loan taken out as an unsecured loan. This will become clearer when I explain the workings of an unsecured loan but it is actually easier to arrange for an unsecured loan to be repaid from the disposal of assets that the borrower owns, rather than liquidating his home or any other specific asset against which the loan was secured, under the terms of a secured personal loan.

A word of advice if you are going down the secured personal loan route, speak to your financial advisor and specifically ask whether it would be better to take out a secured personal loan or a mortgage extension. It may seem to amount to the same thing but in fact it isn't. If you increase your mortgage by say £20,000 in order to buy a car you now have a higher mortgage and a higher repayment, even though the monthly payment is low, as you are using mortgage rates rather than more expensive personal loan and HP rates.

However, if you now miss mortgage payments you put your home at higher risk than if you took out a separate loan secured against the house. In the circumstances you could make the mortgage payments on time and miss a couple of loan payments without the immediate risk of losing your house. Under the rules of the Financial Services Authority you must discuss this situation with your qualified Financial Advisor.

Unsecured Personal Loan

Over the many years that I have been involved in car finance, I believe that the most difficult concept to get across has been contract hire as it includes so many variables. However, by far the most misunderstood is 'unsecured personal loan' because it doesn't 'do what it says on the tin'. The confusion is all in the word 'unsecured' and the fact that unsecured loans attract a lower interest rate than secured loans. Many 'advisors' may tell you otherwise but at the time of writing on the Sainsbury's website an unsecured loan would cost an APR of 7.7% (typical) and a secured homeowner loan 17.9% APR (typical variable)

Logic suggests that if the lender makes a loan that is secured it should be safer than a loan that is unsecured and therefore should be reflected in a lower interest rate. But it isn't. And even using this logic no one seems to question the perceived very high risk attached to an unsecured personal loan.

If you believe that an unsecured personal loan means that nothing you own is at risk – you're nuts!

Saying that a personal loan is "unsecured" is only giving part of the story. A better description is that a loan which is unsecured is secured against nothing in particular. Whenever I have given talks on car finance and the subject of personal loans is raised, audience members always show great support for this method of finance. The reason why this type of loan is so popular is that rather naively, there is a perception that nothing you own is at risk. So what happens if you stop making payments, I usually ask, and the room goes quiet? Do people honestly believe that the funder won't be trying to recover the debt?

Let's be clear – when you take out an unsecured personal loan everything you own, that isn't considered to be an essential, is at risk, including your car and your house. Yes even your house!

One of the most important considerations when taking out any type of finance is to ask what will happen if you don't make your payments? In the case of a secured loan, that is secured against your house, it is unlikely that you will lose your house and certainly not until everything has been done to come up with an alternative way of paying the debt. However, if you default on an unsecured personal loan, the funder, after trying to collect the money owed, will take you to court and get a County Court Judgement issued against you.

You will be expected to make payments as agreed. If you don't make the payments, a bailiff can be appointed and he will try to remove goods from your house, including your car, until he has sufficient to sell in auction in order to pay off your debts including the fees and charges. If the bailiff can't find enough to sell, in order to settle the debt, the lender can use another instrument in order to secure his money, and that is a Charging Order, which, if agreed by the court, registers a charge against your house for the amount still owed. It is not usual for the owner of a house to be forced to sell it in order to satisfy a charging order but it means that when you sell the house the debt will be repaid out the sale proceeds.

As you can probably guess I'm not a big fan of personal loans, not only because of the risk to you and your property but also the loss of legal protection that you would receive if you took out hire purchase. The national press and various so-called experts go on about the low cost of personal loans compared to dealer hire purchase but the fact is that you won't necessarily be offered a personal loan at the rates advertised, making this suggestion misleading. Lenders will assess your financial circumstances and offer you a rate that could be considerably more than the advertised APR.

Whilst the advertised rate must be provided to at least 51% of clients (down from 66% prior to the EU Consumer Credit Directive) this doesn't take account of those who may be a reasonable credit risk but are rejected at application and end up having to choose a lender providing much higher rates. On the other hand, the dealer's HP rate is negotiable and he wants to sell you a car, so negotiate the rates down; you'll find the rates could be much closer to personal loan rates but with HP providing much more legal protection. More of this later.

The greatest benefit of an unsecured personal loan is that it should be cheaper than any other form of finance and you can spend it on anything, including a privately purchased vehicle. You also avoid paying a deposit or advance payment, as you can borrow the full amount required and even include the road fund licence and first year's insurance on the car.

The lender only lends the money based on your ability to repay the debt not on the value of the asset (the car). It is also wise to spread your risk so, if you are going to take out a personal loan, use lender other than your bank, especially if you have other debts such as an overdraft facility with them. As times get tough banks will look at their total exposure to you and they may reduce your overdraft facility.

Whilst your bank knows you best and may be a little more flexible, if you have experienced problems, it is unlikely that they will be any more likely to lend you money than any other lender. Some believe that putting your current account, mortgage, insurances and loans with one source to be the best option. It's not, in fact it's highly risky and, in my opinion, to be avoided.

Hire Purchase

This is still one of the most popular finance methods used by retail buyers and small businesses to spread the cost of their new (or used) car. The car must be supplied by a company and not by a private individual, as the legal responsibility is different between the two should a fault come to light once the car has been purchased. An HP company will need to know that it has legal recourse against the seller, which doesn't exist if the sale is a private transaction. You will often be expected to pay a minimum deposit of 10% of the cost of the car followed by 36 equal monthly instalments over 3 years, 48 over 4 years etc.

You will normally have a documentation fee of up to £150 to pay, either as part of, or in addition to, the deposit (also known as an arrangement fee), with an option to purchase fee at the end of the agreement of around £10 - £50, at which point, should you pay the fee, you will own the car.

Most HP schemes operate on fixed rate interest, in other words you pay a fixed monthly figure to the finance house for the life of the agreement. Variable rate HP is rare these days but still available. It operates in the same way as a variable rate mortgage, whereby if interest rates go up, so do your repayments and if they go down, your repayments go down also. Using this type of HP makes it difficult to compare lenders as you can't predict the future.

Over the past few years, where rates have dropped, variable rate would have been a good option but, at times when rates are unpredictable, and as likely to increase as decrease, it would be wiser to opt for a fixed rate if you are given a choice. In 2012/13 with interest rates at an all time low only take fixed rate as interest rates can only go one way in the future – up!

Hire purchase is a purchase scheme so ownership is an option but, legally, you do not own the vehicle until you have made your last payment and, if required, paid the nominal option to purchase fee. Until you have made the final option to purchase payment you are simply hiring it – get it? Hire Purchase.

It is for reasons of title that the law changed to involve the lender in any dispute between you and the supplying dealer and/or the manufacturer. In the past if you believed that you had been supplied faulty goods or the supplier misrepresented the goods, you were left to tackle the suppliers alone but the funder would still expect you to pay on time, even though you may not be able to drive the vehicle.

However, closer inspection of section 75 of the Consumer Credit Act shows that, in many cases, the funder shares equal liability with the supplier and you can sue him over faulty goods, misrepresentation, etc. More of this later in the section 'What to do when things go wrong'. In essence it means that, should you experience problems with the vehicle or the way that it was sold to you, you have more power over the supplier by taking hire purchase than by paying cash. This legal advantage is extremely important as it can also save you a substantial amount of money.

There are other legal issues that are covered later in this book in the section 'What to do when things go wrong'.

Hire purchase is the simplest way of spreading your costs and you can calculate your monthly payments with a calculator yourself using the quoted flat rate (not APR). Let's say that after paying your deposit you have £10,000 to finance over three years at 5% flat. The interest calculation is simply £10,000 x 5% = £500 per annum, so over 3 years the interest would be £500 x 3 = £1,500. If you add this on to the capital figure of £10,000 and divide by 36, this would be your monthly repayments, ie. £10,000 plus £1,500 = £11,500 divided by 36 = £319.40. Similarly for four years the figures are: £10,000 plus £2,000 interest = £12,000 divided by 48 = £250. Knowing how to calculate the figures is useful and easy when using a flat rate but how can you compare different schemes?

You need to know the annual percentage rate (APR) which is far more complicated to calculate. Where the transaction falls within the Consumer Credit Act (this will be identified at the top of the agreement as 'regulated') you must have the APR shown. Other than spreading the cost of finance and incurring interest charges, there is little to choose between HP and cash purchase when it comes to negotiating a purchase price.

You can only negotiate with the dealer within the bounds of the available dealer discount and the amount that he wants to retain as profit in the car. You will also have to dispose of the vehicle at the end of the agreement, although you may be able to benefit from subsidized or 0% interest rate from the dealer – but take care that you haven't paid for the subsidy within the price you pay for the car.

It is possible to negotiate a better deal on any part exchange or free extras if the dealer is making an additional profit out of the finance arrangement and, as the HP rate to the dealer is normally fairly similar to the average personal loan rate, try to negotiate the rate down. He often receives an override bonus based on volume of new car business financed so, in fact, he could provide the finance at cost just to get him closer to the bonus threshold.

If you would like a rough guide to calculating the APR from a flat rate, try the following: Flat Rate x 2 x 90%. So a flat rate of 7% would be an APR of 12.6% (7 x 2 x 90% = 12.6). The actual rate is 12.8% based on a loan of £10,000 over 3 years. This is just a guide and is not meant to be as accurate as the true figure but gives a pretty reasonable indicator. Always make sure that, if you are comparing rates, you compare APR with APR or flat rate with flat rate. Many dealers have reverted to quoting flat rate in order to con you into believing it is an APR.

Your legal rights are much stronger with HP than personal loans. Provided the deal falls within the Consumer Credit Act, the car cannot be repossessed without a court order once you have paid a third of the total amount owing. The huge benefit, and one that could save you £000's, is your right to terminate your agreement once you have paid half the total amount owed without any additional payments, known as the 50% rule or Voluntary Termination (VT), sections 99 and 100 of the Consumer Credit Act.

This is costing the finance industry over £100 million per annum and increasing as more consumers become aware of their legal rights. In the current climate, if you wanted to change your car before the end of the agreement there is a good chance that you will be 'upside down' or in negative equity. In other words you will owe more to the lender than the car is worth.

However, if you have paid more than 50% of the total amount owed (as shown under 'Termination Your Rights' on the front page of the agreement), you can simply contact the lender and tell them you want to voluntarily terminate your agreement. Put it in writing and hand back the car. On average this is saving drivers around £2,500. I always recommend that you take legal advice before exercising your right to VT your car, as a note will appear on your credit file to show that you have exercised your right to VT the car. This is a legal entitlement, you are doing nothing wrong, but if you do it several times it will put a lender off and may affect your ability to obtain finance in the future.

VAT: When you take out HP on a new car the VAT will be added to the cost of the car to arrive at a purchase price. The same applies if you finance a used car that is what's known as VAT qualifying, the VAT is included in the purchase price. However, if you were to lease the same car, the purchase price to the leasing company would be the figure excluding the VAT, thereby making the purchase price less. If you are a business it may be worth considering leasing because whilst you pay VAT on the monthly payments you can recover 50% of this payment (if you are VAT registered) as well as only paying interest on the purchase price excluding the VAT.

Important Note: I don't want to confuse anyone here but really just for information I felt I should mention the following: a new EU Consumer Credit Directive was voted in on 17th January 2008 by the European Parliament. The new directive was aimed at harmonizing consumer credit laws throughout member states whilst maintaining a high level of consumer protection. Final regulations were produced in December 2009 and implemented in May 2010. There will be early repayment provisions within the new regulations allowing the debtor (the person that borrows the money) to pay back the debt in part or full at any time and without notice but section 99 of the Consumer Credit Act, allowing consumers to VT their agreement, will no longer apply to Conditional Sale Agreements but will still apply to Hire Purchase agreements. This is likely to result in lenders moving away from the potential losses attached to HP and onto Conditional Sale agreements, which will remove some of the attractiveness of this type of arrangement. If you are taking out an agreement check your agreement, it could be critical. Make sure that if it falls within the Consumer Credit Act the agreement includes your right to VT the agreements. This also applies to PCP. Read my blog at http://www.thebestcarfinanceblog.co.uk for regular updates.

Personal Contract Purchase (PCP)

This is rapidly becoming the most popular method of purchasing a new or nearly new car, mainly because it combines many advantages with few disadvantages. In essence it works like HP but with a final deferred, or balloon, payment that should equate to the expected sales value of the car at the end of the agreement, based on your anticipated mileage. You then have the option to purchase the vehicle at the end of the agreement, at the predetermined price, or simply hand it back to the leasing company.

If the car is valued higher than the "option to purchase" figure, quoted on the agreement, you can buy the car then sell it on for a profit. On the other hand if the car isn't worth the final settlement figure you can simply hand the car back to the leasing company, although you will have to pay for any excess miles, over the agreed total contract mileage, at an agreed pence per mile rate, as shown on the contract, along with any unrepaired accident damage. It's a win win situation for you. If the car is handed back, because it isn't worth the final figure, it means that the funder has miscalculated the final figure and he must bear the loss.

Clearly, if the figure had been set lower in the first place, the monthly cost would have been higher, so you are actually better off because you've ended up paying less than if you'd have taken HP and carried the loss yourself. When you arrange for a quote from the dealer, broker or finance house you must decide how long you want to keep the car for – three years is normally the optimum, as you will be handing the car back just as it is due to have an MOT test and, for many cars, the end of its warranty. Next you must estimate the annual mileage, this must be as near to your actual mileage as you can get. You should check to see if you can alter the mileage part way through the contract, which in turn will adjust the monthly payments and final payment to reflect the higher or lower mileage. Finally, you need to decide if you would like to include a maintenance package. These maintenance packages can vary so check that all service and maintenance costs are included. Including parts, labour, tyres, batteries and exhausts.

Check for restrictions such as where you can have your car serviced and where you can have replacement tyres fitted. If you have a maintenance package always call the maintenance hotline before having work carried out as they will need to authorize it.

You should be aware of some of the mechanics of the PCP and what to be cautious of. First of all you actually enter into two agreements in one. The first is for the finance with a balloon payment that must be paid at the end of the contract.

The second part is where you appoint the funder or his agent to sell the vehicle on your behalf and to pay the amount due in your agreement; they sustain any losses but also retain any profits. This is where things could go wrong. To illustrate how things could go wrong, one of our customers arranged a PCP through us using a manufacturer's own PCP. She was a legal secretary and inspected every detail of the agreement, only to find that when the car was sold on her behalf at the end of the agreement, by the supplying dealer, who acted as agent, if the agent sustained a loss she would have to make good the difference between the final balloon figure and the price achieved. After much discussion she received a letter to confirm that she would not receive this charge and the contract was altered for future deals, so the lesson here is: CHECK YOUR CONTRACT - NOT ALL MAY BE AS IT APPEARS OR AS EXPLAINED!

Many people get confused over the comparisons between the APR on HP agreements to that shown on a PCP agreement, when you look at the amount of actual interest paid. You can have the same price of car financed on HP and PCP with identical APR's and yet pay more interest with a PCP but with lower monthly payments. Confused? You will be because I am about to explain!

PCP Calculations: Let's look at a £10,000 car expected to be worth £4,000 in three years time. We are looking at two distinct calculations. The loan is split into two parts. The first part is the £4,000 final payment. We are deferring this payment to the end of the agreement so none of this amount is repaid during the agreement, you will be paying interest only throughout the agreements as you're not paying off any of the £4,000. The other portion, ie. £6,000, is paid off with interest throughout the loan term, like a straightforward HP agreement. The figures shown below have been simplified for illustration purposes and ease of explanation but they are sufficiently accurate for this exercise:

We have two calculations here. The first is the interest only payment on the deferred payment of £4,000, as follows:

£4,000 x 9.5% (APR) = £380 (We have used APR as this is close to the annual rate when paying interest only)

Total interest over 3 years = £380 x 3 = £1,140

The second calculation is the repayment calculation of the balance of the advance, ie. £6,000. The interest is calculated using the flat rate of 5% (roughly the equivalent to an APR of 9.5%).

Please note that the figures shown are not completely accurate, they are simply to illustrate the mechanics of the calculations.

£6,000 x 5% = £300

Total interest over 3 years = £300 x 3 = £900

The total repaid over 3 years before the deferred (optional) payment is as follows:

Interest on £4,000 deferred payment	£1,140
Capital repaid	£6,000
Interest on capital	£ 900
Total repaid before deferred payment	£8,040

Represented by:

36 monthly payments x **£223.33**

(total interest paid £1,140 + £900 = £2,040)

If you compare this to a straight forward HP with a similar interest rate of 5% flat (equivalent to 9.5% APR) the calculation would be:

£10,000 x 5% = £500 per annum

The total interest over 3 years will be £500 x 3 = £1,500

Total repayment:

Total Interest	£ 1,500
Capital repaid	£10,000
Total repaid with HP	£11,500
	======

Represented by:

36 monthly payments x **£319.44**

(total interest paid = £1,500)

So, in summary, whilst the APR may be the same, the actual amount of interest you pay with a PCP is greater than an HP agreement, but your monthly cost would be less with a PCP and you will be much better off if the car is worth less at the end of the agreement than the amount allowed for in the PCP agreement. <u>My recommendation is to take out the risk and keep monthly payments down by opting for a PCP.</u>

Contract Hire & Personal Contract Hire (PCH)

This scheme is for consumers and businesses and operates exactly the same for both; however, I have touched on a few small variances for consumers under the heading of personal contract hire (PCH). I'll include the main principles here.

Imagine hiring a car from your local car rental company for a week but, instead of keeping it for a week, you keep it for three years before you give it back. That is the equivalent to contract hire, which can be provided to businesses and to private individuals or consumers. You never actually own the vehicle you simply rent it at a fixed monthly cost based on your anticipated annual mileage. If you exceed the mileage you will be charged a fee at the end of the contract, expressed as pence per mile, for the distance that you cover over the contract allowance.

Most contract hire companies will allow you to adjust your monthly payments if you find that you are covering substantially more or less miles than the original estimated mileage. You may be restricted to one change throughout the contract period so be realistic if you change. Adjusting your monthly payment will normally work out less than paying the excess mileage charge at the end of the agreement. Check with whoever you lease the car from that you are able to amend the monthly payment during the contract to reflect any change in mileage from the contracted mileage. Ask if you can increase and decrease the monthly payments and how many times you are allowed to do this throughout the lease term?

As with PCP, the quotes are computer generated and depend on the price of the car, after allowing for discounts and bonuses, the resale value based on the contract term, your anticipated mileage, interest charges and administration costs. Rates can vary dramatically between suppliers as they all have different purchase terms with the dealers and manufacturers, they will also calculate residual values differently (ie. the expected value at the end of the contract) and cost of funds can vary (this is the interest that the leasing company has to pay on the money that it uses to lend to its customers).

If the contract hire company is bank owned, their money is cheaper than an independent that has to buy in its funds from a finance institution. To illustrate how rates can vary, for not so obvious reasons, one contract hire company, for whom I provided consultancy services, was owned by a Toyota dealership network. Toyotas were therefore bought cheaper by their own contract hire company than any other, much larger, contract hire company could buy them.

As the dealership group had retail sites, through which they could sell the end of contract cars for more money, they could set the residual (resale) values higher, making the vehicles cheaper than all of their larger competitors, even after allowing for the higher interest that they had to pay for their funds. So, nothing is quite as it seems with contract hire as there are so many variables. There are many great advantages to contract hire for businesses and consumers. For example:

Cost of vehicle:

As you are only renting the vehicle at a fixed monthly charge, you are never told the actual cost of the vehicle. You are, therefore, more likely to be the beneficiary of additional manufacturer's bonuses as you are not aware (nor will any of those buying end of contract cars) of the actual price paid for the car by the contract hire company. These low purchase prices will, therefore, not affect the used car prices on dealership forecourts.

The contract hire companies often factor into their calculations £'000's of manufacturers bonuses passing the benefits on to you. **Misunderstanding 1: It is better to buy a used or ex demonstrator car after it has lost its initial depreciation.** This can be the case but we know that manufactures often give away much more in bonuses to leasing companies on a new car than the first year's depreciation on a used car. We have a recent example where a French manufacturer was providing new cars with a retail cost of £20,010 to leasing companies for £11,595, delivered by a main dealer to the front door of the customer. It is these deals that make leasing a great alternative and my favourite form of car finance. You should also note that the RAC annual cost of motoring 2010 showed it costs, on average, £553 per annum more to run a used, 3 year old car than a brand new car.

To illustrate how much profit manufacturers still have in their cars to play with, we simply have to compare our prices with the Unites States. I have illustrated this in a video which you can view by going to:

http://www.videotrainingonthenet.com/leasetrainingUSprices2.html

Sourcing the vehicles:

Either the broker that you use, or the contract hire company that provides the finance, will have special terms and maximum discount arranged with their preferred supplying dealerships, so the car of your choice will be sourced for you and delivered to you anywhere in the UK. You simply place an order. On the other hand you could visit your local dealer and check out his rates, although not all will provide PCH.

Dealers are not always as competitive unless they have set up their own broker operation, giving them access to a number of contract hire companies with competitive rates. Not everyone likes to haggle over prices so this is great if this applies to you as the best price has already been negotiated for you and included in the rate.

Disposing of the vehicle:

At the end of the contract you will normally receive a telephone call from the contract hire company in order to arrange collection of the car, which will then be sent to auction or sold via one of their other sales routes. They will pick up your car at your convenience at an agreed time and place. Quite painless with no risk to you, especially at times when used car prices are fluctuating badly. If you decide that you would like to keep the vehicle you can always offer to buy it.

Have a figure in mind as they will often ask you for an offer. Offer the trade value, as you can always increase your offer when they start to fall about in hysterical laughter, but bear in mind that they are only expecting to reach trade price in auction and they have the added expense of inspecting the vehicle, collecting the vehicle, preparing it, auction costs and administration costs. They could end up with £1,000 or more under the trade value that you are offering, so battle hard. Beware, we have heard of a few incidents where clients have been told that they must pay for the collection of the end of contract vehicle, this may be yet another way for those companies that slash their rates to recover some of their lost profit from you.

Road fund licence (Car Tax):

With contract hire the car is registered in the name of the contract hire company so they must pay for the road fund licence. The good news for you is that you therefore do not have that cost to bear. But beware, some contract hire companies have been known to recharge the cost to you if it has not been allowed in the rate, check your contract.

Mercedes are famous for providing cars on a simple form of contract hire, known as an operating lease, which normally means you only have the first year's road fund licence paid for in the contract. You will have to pay for subsequent years, which can be quite expensive so check your contract.

Financial:

First of all, in the current climate, it is wise for businesses and consumers to spread their risk. Using an overdraft for buying cars is foolish and to use your bank would be even more daft, as banks are becoming tougher all the time and using your available overdraft this way would reduce the amount of credit available for other purposes. So it would be much better to spread your borrowing/finance requirements as wide as possible. Hence, using an independent leasing company would be wiser.

For businesses there are benefits attached to off balance sheet funding, which is what contract hire is. In other words, you don't show vehicles on the balance sheet nor do you show the outstanding debt as a liability, so this type of funding can strengthen the company's gearing and give it greater worth. However, companies should be cautious if this is a major deciding factor, as the accounting rules look set to change with vehicles on contract hire expected to be accounted for on the balance sheet.

More information on my blog:

www.thebestcarfinanceblog.co.uk as new accounting standard changes are adopted.

There was also a change, effective from 6th April 2009, that improved the amount of tax write off you can incorporate into your profit and loss, especially when accounting for expensive cars.

Previously, the percentage of the monthly rental that was disallowed increased as the car became more expensive over £12,000, up to a maximum of 25%. From 6th April 2009 this changed and all cars with CO_2 emissions less than 160g/km were to have the full rental written off against tax, whilst over 160g/km the tax disallowance was capped at 15%. In other words, if you are paying £200 + VAT per month you can only set off £170 per month

(85%) against tax if the car emits 161g/km or more CO_2 gas.

Always check on the current rules before committing to a car as major changes are in the pipeline.

Cash flow is much more predictable and if you include a maintenance package you can also spread the cost of service and maintenance evenly over the lease period. The service and maintenance portion of the rental is 100% offset for tax purposes if you are a business user.

VAT

Misunderstanding 2: Contract hire is no good for you unless you are VAT registered.

This is one of the most common misunderstandings when I discuss leasing with business users, as they believe that if you take a purchase product, such as HP, you don't pay VAT. This is wrong, in fact you not only pay VAT on the purchase price of the vehicle you also pay interest on the VAT content. Let me explain.

With contract hire the leasing company can reclaim all of the VAT paid on the purchase price of the car because, as far as they and the Revenue are concerned, the car is purchased solely for business use. This means that a car that costs £10,000 + VAT only costs the leasing company £10,000. So, when they calculate the lease rate, they apply interest charges to the £10,000 but end up with a rate that has VAT applied. If you are not VAT registered, this means that you cannot reclaim any of the VAT that you pay on the monthly payment - but you actually save money because you are not being charged interest on the VAT content of the car cost.

Let's compare this with a purchase scheme such as HP. HP rules do not allow the lender to reclaim any part of the VAT, so whilst the car costs the same, ie. £10,000 + VAT, the lender now has to add in the VAT making a total of £12,000 on which interest is calculated. So, whilst you don't pay any VAT on your monthly payments, it has already been factored into the purchase price of the car and you end up paying interest on the VAT content. So you see **you are better off with contract hire than a purchase scheme even when you are not VAT registered.** Note: This only applies to new cars unless, as mentioned above, the used car that you are financing is what's known as VAT qualifying. VAT qualifying means that the lender can reclaim the VAT content of the purchase price of the car.

Maintenance:

This is an option with all types of finance, even cash purchase. If you are covering higher mileage it is a good option to consider – it helps to spread the cost and it can save money. But look closely at what you are getting for your money. Even if you are only covering low mileage it can still be of benefit.

I remember when I was married my wife was driving less than 10,000 miles per annum but, even so, I was pleased that I put her car on a full maintenance agreement because, instead of me becoming her personal transport manager, having to investigate every minor problem with her car, she sent the service manager at the local main dealer totally insane instead! Worth every penny of the additional cost of maintenance in my book and, as I'm sure you understand, full maintenance on my wife's car probably saved my marriage for many years!

In terms of cost, the optimum mileage at which you should consider a maintenance contract increases as service intervals become greater. My recommendation is, in most cases, 20,000 miles per annum.

The contract hire companies make a fixed charge simply for administering your maintenance account, this can range from £7 to £30 per month before accounting for labour and material costs of servicing. They pass on virtually all the savings that they achieve in terms of reduced labour costs and discounted parts such as tyres, but these savings can be eliminated after accounting for the administration charges; so you should consider the options very carefully.

Insurance:

Whenever you take out finance on a car it is always wise to take out fully comprehensive insurance. In the case of contract hire, it is a contractual term that you take out fully comprehensive insurance. You should also make sure that it covers you for business use if you will be using the car for business.

If you don't and an investigator or loss adjuster finds out that you were on business, when involved in the accident, this may invalidate your insurance or may cause the insurance company not to make a full payout. If the insurance company knows that the car is leased, they may make the payout direct to the leasing company in the case of a total write off.

In the early part of the agreement you may find that the insurance payout wouldn't be enough to cover the settlement cost of your car, in the event of a write off. You should, therefore, consider taking out some GAP Insurance (general asset protection insurance). This will pay the difference between what you owe the leasing company and how much the insurance company will pay out. Check the terms of the GAP insurance before taking it out as some simply pay the difference between the settlement figure and what the car is worth, whilst others pay the difference between the settlement figure and the original invoice cost of the car, known as 'back to invoice' GAP.

Risk:

It seems that the highest risks in contract hire are in two places; the end of contract condition and termination costs if you need to terminate the agreement early. Some contract hire providers, especially those that buy your business by offering the cheapest rates, look to end of contract charges as a way to recoup any losses or improve their profit. After allowing for costs, most people would be surprised to learn that leasing companies make an average of £625 net profit on each lease. So, if they lose £1,000 on a car in auction, against the anticipated sale value, they lose all the profit in the deal – it is hardly surprising, therefore, that they make exorbitant charges at the end of the contract in an attempt to return to profit.

Make sure that you have the car carefully checked by a bodyshop for any damage, over and above normal wear and tear; make sure that the service book is stamped up to date (you will be charged a penalty if it isn't); return all keys and instruction books etc. It is also wise to have photos taken of each panel of the vehicle, using a non digital camera, and get an independent witness sign each photo as being a true picture in the event that you have a dispute over end of contract condition with the leasing company.

This may sound excessive but I have had complaints from people who have bought my book, 'An Insider Guide To Car Finance' who have had end of contract charges in excess of £4,000. That would make the £10 per month saving, achieved by using the cheapest company, a bit of a false saving. You should note that it is now possible to insure yourself against end of contract charges. I have written about it in my blog, www.thebestcarfinanceblog.co.uk

The other main problem with contract hire arises if you need to terminate the agreement early because you need to change the car, or your circumstances change. Many mainstream funders will charge a flat 50% of all outstanding rentals from the date of termination, others will charge a scale, say 60% of rentals outstanding in year one, 50% in year two and 40% in year three of a three year contract.

However, others are simply crooks – I heard recently of a situation whereby the client was expected to pay 95% of outstanding rentals in year two of a three year contract – so my advice, if you only want the car for two years, is to just take out a two year agreement. In the case of the sensible companies, you will still normally be in pocket after returning the car early and paying the termination fee, compared to taking the car on hire purchase with higher monthly payments and losing the difference between what the HP company wants as a settlement and what the car is worth at the time you terminate.

Important Note: If you have to terminate your contract hire agreement early please remember that the leasing company can only recover its costs and cannot charge what amounts to a penalty. Legal precedent was set in the case of Volkswagen Financial Services (UK) Ltd v George Ramage. Mr Ramage had a 3 year hire agreement (contract hire) with VW Financial Services.

Shortly after his first anniversary of the agreement he fell into arrears, following which the car was repossessed. VWFS then sued Mr. Ramage for a money judgment in accordance with the relevant terms of the agreement.

The term stated that the hirer was liable for the total amount of the rentals payable during the hire period less the amount of the rentals paid and less also a small rebate (4 percent) on the rentals that had not become due.

After going to appeal HHJ Sennitt held that the terms did not provide for a genuine pre-estimate of loss and was therefore a penalty and unenforceable. There were other reasons why the judge reached his conclusion with references to other legal precedents and other factors such as road fund licence unused and breakdown recovery unused.

In essence if you feel that you are being overcharged as a result of an early termination of your agreement write to the leasing company citing the VWFS v Ramage case and ask that they re – consider. If they refuse you can complain to the Office of Fair Trading or the Financial Ombudsman Service. They will give you guidance.

If you are one of my customers I provide letters to write and courses of action to follow, as should any good broker. Don't expect this level of expert support from bucket shop type lease providers, dealers or when dealing direct with the leasing companies themselves. They tend not to have the time, expertise or inclination to help.

To summarize, contract hire is virtually risk-free, provided you stick to the contract conditions. It is probably the most convenient way of driving a car, which is really all you want to do. If only we could all focus our minds away from the British obsession to own things, we could all end up driving better cars whilst saving money at the same time. As I say in my lectures, would you still want to own your house if its value dropped by 60% in 3 years? Because that's what most people experience when they buy many new cars for cash or on HP.

Personal Contract Hire

Please read the section on contract hire to understand the mechanics of the product along with the advantages and disadvantages.

Some funders will not provide contract hire to non business users, whilst others charge a premium of a few pounds per month to consumers, over and above the business rates. In all cases you must add VAT to the monthly figures and initial payments. Having said this, as an individual, you can achieve huge savings by using contract hire and often achieve rates that match the rates paid by some of the largest fleets in the UK.

However, you must be very wary of end of contract charges. For example, some funders will charge twice the excess mileage rates to a consumer compared to business. They may also step the charge by charging one rate if you cover up to 10% more than the contracted mileage and up to double this rate for any mileage over the 10% figure.

For example, let's say you contract to cover 10,000 miles per annum over three years, that's a total of 30,000 miles. But you cover 36,000 miles. You may have to pay 5 pence per mile for the first 3,000 miles (10%) then 10 pence per mile thereafter making your excess mileage charge:

3,000 miles x £0.05	£150
3,000 miles x £0.10	£300
Total	£450 + VAT

Business users are more likely to pay a flat 5 pence per mile. There seems to be no logical reason for this, other than the belief that consumers are more gullible than business users. Experience also shows that consumers are more likely to receive excessive repair and end of contract charges for the same reason. In order to see how you can avoid these charges see the section above on contract hire.

Contract Hire for consumers (PCH) is still great, even with the slightly higher rentals and, if you are selective, you can save a fortune. Beware of the VAT content. Some brokers that quote VAT inclusive rates for consumers don't make you aware that the VAT rate that you pay is the rate ruling when you actually make your payments (each month), not the rate ruling when you took out your contract. This caused massive confusion when the standard rate increased from 17.5% to 20%. Don't get caught out.

Section 3: What To Do When Things Go Wrong Part 1

General Advice

In the last recession I lost my business. It was successful and expanding at the time but in order to fund the expansion of our business we took a substantial investment from one of my main customers. Following a bizarre series of events our investor lost everything, which, in turn, also destroyed my business. I lost everything, my house and my business along with my family and my self esteem. But here I am today, still alive and kicking with grown up children working my way through the current recession.

The point is that I have suffered what many are going through at the moment. I know what it's like to lose everything, have creditors knocking on the door and suffering sleepless nights. But if I had known then what I know now, I may even have managed to keep my house and possibly kept my business trading. So, in this next section, I'm going to try to make any problems you have as painless as possible and share with you the one piece of advice that will make all the problems manageable.

The most important thing to remember is that when things go wrong in your life, maybe even if you feel it was your fault or you made a bad judgement, it doesn't make you a bad person. It simply makes you a person with a problem that needs solving and believe me there are plenty of people out there who want to help you. YOU ARE NOT ALONE!

Having a problem with your finances can be brought about by many things, sickness, divorce or separation, loss of a job or business, accident, loss of a friend or family member; sometimes it follows something amazingly good like a marriage, birth of a child or moving to a bigger house, creating lots of unexpected costs and overstretching you beyond your income.

Whatever the cause, the effect is the same – misery. Unless, of course, you know how to deal with the situation and from whom you can get advice and support. So, having experienced the nightmare myself, I'm going to give you as much advice and resource as I possibly can to relieve the problem. I want my advice to be the most helpful you can get and, whilst it is aimed at resolving problems with your car finance, I hope it will enable you to deal with all your debt problems in a constructive way.

I'm going to cover these things in detail later but for now I want to enforce upon you the need to do 2 things. The first is – keep a diary. Note all the events leading up to the point of getting into debt and everything that happens thereafter. Note down when you receive letters and when you respond and keep all correspondence in a file for future reference.

Every time you speak to someone on the phone make a note of the date, time and details of the conversation and always get a note of the name of the person to whom you were talking, this is most important if you agree to do something yourself or the lender agrees to a course of action. Keep copies of emails sent and received. If you agree something on the telephone, always confirm what was agreed in a letter. You want no misunderstandings on either side and keeping this level of information may prevent a lender attempting to take you to court. The second thing, and one that I failed to do when I had problems, is COMMUNICATE.

Don't put bills in a drawer and think they will go away – trust me, they won't. I did this and learned to my cost that things can only get worse. You must get in touch with the people to whom you owe money immediately – let them know that you are having problems and you are trying to sort them out! If you get in touch early enough you may be able to come to an arrangement that may not even find its way onto your credit file, keeping your credit clean.

If you don't get in touch, you can guarantee that your file will show arrears and possibly defaults which, as I will explain, are really bad news when you want to move forward. So in summary, keep a diary and communicate, and if you are frightened of discussing things on the phone you can insist that all contact is in writing and, as I'll explain, there are people to communicate for you. **Just don't worry!**

Let's get back to car finance. Do you have any payment protection insurance (PPI)? Some people took it out at the time of taking out the agreement for finance without realising that they have been talked into it by a slick car salesman or broker. In fact, if you have a financial problem, you may find that Mr Slick has done you a favour. If you have PPI check the terms carefully to see if you are covered for your circumstances. PPI can cover accident, sickness, redundancy and death.

They can cover just one, all, or any permutation, depending on the policy and the payments you have made. You are normally only covered for a limited number of months so, if you are made redundant, you can normally only claim for 12 months repayments of your loan or finance agreement, even though the loan may be over 5 years. Again, check your policy carefully. If you feel you are covered, contact the insurer, he will have a claims procedure which can often be completed online or even over the phone, although from personal experience I would try to keep everything in writing.

If you were sold the policy believing that you were covered for all circumstances only to find that you're not, you may have a claim against the insurer. There have been many cases of PPI miss-selling, resulting in the insurer being forced to pay the claims as well as pay compensation. You should complain to the Financial Ombudsman Service (details at the end of the book). If you are reading this just to see what can go wrong, I would strongly suggest that you consider some form of Payment Protection Insurance, now pretty much replaced by Income Protection Insurance. The law has been tightened to avoid miss-selling of financial services products so you won't get stung as you may have been in the past.

You have to take out your policy after you have arranged the finance, it can no longer be arranged at the same time. Make sure that the payments are linked to the loan repayments and cease becoming payable if you pay off the loan. Many people have found that they have a 5 year PPI policy to run alongside a 5 year car loan but, when they change the car after say 3 years and settle the finance, they still have a further 2 years of payment protection to pay. Make sure you can stop PPI payments when you settle your finance.

Another problem that can lead to financial difficulties is a major accident resulting in your car being a total write off. Most people believe that the insurance payout will simply pay the finance company what is owed, possibly leaving some money over. In truth, depending on how far you are into the finance agreement, you may find yourself with more to pay the finance company than the insurance company is willing to pay for your loss.

This is often the case in the early stages of a PCP or early into a long HP agreement. There is an insurance policy that will cover this shortfall and some lenders include it as part of your agreement so, again, it is worth checking to see if it has been included. The insurance is called GAP insurance (General Asset Protection). Even if you have fully comprehensive insurance, which you must have if you have finance secured against the car, if your car is written off you may find the insurance payout doesn't match the settlement figure provided by the finance company.

If you have taken out HP and paid a large deposit, there is unlikely to be a negative difference. However, if you have a PCP or Contract Hire/PCH you are more likely to have a difference to pay, which can run into several £000's early into the agreement. If you don't have GAP insurance, you must discuss the shortfall with the lender and come to an arrangement to pay the difference or risk having adverse information recorded on your credit file just as you need to arrange finance for a replacement car.

Case History: Just to put the level of shortfall into perspective, one of my clients had an Audi A3 that was being driven by one of his managers. The car was written off in an accident which was the fault of his manager just 6 months after he took delivery. Following the insurance claim there was a shortfall of £3,000 between the insurance payout and the amount required by the leasing company. As there was no GAP insurance in existence I arranged for the insurance company to talk to the leasing company. Whilst they agreed a better figure, which amounted to a reduction of £1,500, it still left my client with the £1,500 to pay. Lesson learned.

OK, assuming that you haven't got PPI and you haven't written the car off, what do you need to do to minimise the pain of running into financial problems? There were many lessons learned in the last recession, laws are now different and there is a great deal of support about. Debt collectors have to stick to a code of conduct and you even have protection against loan sharks if you have gone down that route in desperation.

Let me remind you of one essential thing you must do, repeated 3 times to emphasise the importance:

COMMUNICATE, COMMUNICATE, COMMUNICATE.

I remember receiving demands from the bank and credit card companies and sticking the letters in a drawer. I remember the drawer, it was the one I couldn't see when I went into the kitchen. But as I found out, debts don't go away because you can no longer see the demand letters from those you owe money to. In fact they just get worse.

Let's say you lend a friend some money and he promises to pay you back when he gets paid at the end of the month. It gets to the end of the month and you don't hear from him. A further week goes by and you still don't hear from him. How do you feel? Are you angry? Do you feel let down? If you are anything like me you will be. In fact I'd be spitting bullets. But in fact at the end of the month your friend was made redundant but you weren't to know.

Let's say that, instead of avoiding you, he phoned and said that he has been made redundant and is desperately looking for a job but that he may struggle to pay you back all the money he owes you. If he offers to pay you some money out of his redundancy, the chances are that you will tell him not to worry and to pay you back when he can afford to. The situation is the same, he still owes you all the money, but you can now forget it until he lets you know he can pay you. And he no longer has to worry about the debt that he can't currently afford to repay.

Now whilst you will be dealing with large companies, the people you are dealing with are human and if you call and explain your situation they will normally try to help. So my advice is to treat your debts as personal and always ask the person at the other end of the phone for help, people feel good about helping others in trouble. And remember, you are one of thousands that they are dealing with, as soon as they know your circumstances and can deal with the problem they can get back to trying to contact those that have stuffed the demands in a drawer.

It is important to get in quick and ask for help before things get serious. I have always found it easier to negotiate with a lender than a debt collector, which is where your debt will end up if you don't make your payments and don't communicate.

Before moving away from the need to communicate, if you have a problem talking to people about debt on the phone, you can always write and ask the company to whom you owe the money, to communicate in writing only. There is also a lot of help available, which I will come onto in a moment. You are not alone with debt problems these days as I was in the 90's.

The first thing you need to do is prepare an income and expenditure account. Establish what your household income is including tax credits, child allowance etc. Then list all of your monthly expenditure, including mortgage/rent, council tax, telephone, utilities, television licence, food, car costs, loans etc. This will help to put your debt into perspective and allow you to prioritise your debt payments.

If you are confused by your debt then you need help from one of the help agencies. Some are run by the government and others are 'not for profit' institutions. However, there are some that only want to make money out of your problems. They either try to push you to consolidate your debt into a new loan that they arrange, or they are recommended by a company to whom you owe money.

You receive a letter from the company to whom you owe money, in which they recommend using such a credit advice company, giving the impression that they will help you with all your debts. In fact their help will be biased towards repaying the debt to this one creditor (the company you owe the money to), as they are tied to this company and they earn a commission for collecting all or some of the money you owe.

Always use the government agencies or not for profit agencies, they should always be able to give you independent and unbiased advice about dealing with all of your debt. I've listed them at the end of this book.

Prioritise Your Debt

Once you have made a list of your debt, you need to prioritise it, you can do this yourself or with the help of a debt counsellor. You need to make sure that you pay debts that could result in a prison sentence such as council tax, first.

The good news is that if you are made redundant your council tax is paid for you. You need to make sure that you keep a roof over your head. The government has introduced provisions to make it more difficult for your home to be repossessed – if you fall behind with mortgage payments, take advice from your lender and your financial advisor.

You may be able to get all or part of your mortgage repayments paid for you if you are unemployed, talk to your local housing benefits office or take advice from your debt counsellor. Of course, for the purposes of this book, I'm mainly concerned about the finance used to fund your car. You may be able to do without your car, in which case we will look at ways you can surrender it. More of this later.

Your Broker

A professional broker will try to help you and look after you when you find yourself in difficulties. Unfortunately, many people use the online bucket shops, who generally don't have the experience, knowledge or inclination to help, so you are very much on your own. In order to provide low rates, they often use funders who are less tolerant, as their margins are very thin, when customers run into arrears or experience difficulties.

You may also find them hard to deal with, making it essential that you deal with them through a debt councillor. It is the risk you take when you use the online bucket shops. A good broker will not only provide advice but may also make representation to the funder on your behalf, reducing some of the pressure.

Making Contact

Do this as quickly as possible, preferably before you go into arrears. Have your income and expenditure calculations in front of you when you make the call so that you can discuss what you have available and what you can afford to pay. Most lenders will be pleased that you have contacted them but really haven't got the time to listen to the whole history of the problems you face, be precise and brief then make your offer.

Try not to get caught up in a negotiation, as some lenders employ professionals who will try to get you to commit to more than you can afford, which in my opinion is wrong. Be precise and make the offer a figure that you know you can afford without causing excessive hardship. Your objective may well be to keep your car but not at the cost of starving. Oh, and don't make false promises to increase your payments in a couple of months unless you know you will be able to.

Learn to bite your tongue. The best negotiators actually say the least, make your offer and SHUT UP. The best form of contact is in writing. Keep copies of what you have sent and received back. When you speak to someone make sure you make a note of the date and time of the call and exactly what was said, don't rely upon your memory – this is often one of the biggest mistakes causing an unnecessary dispute later. As I mentioned earlier, keep a diary.

When you make an offer make it as high as you can comfortably afford but don't worry if this amount is small, it is better than nothing. By making contact and an offer it shows the creditor (the company to whom you owe the money) that you are serious about sorting out the problem. It will also help your case if you end up in court but by using the right approach you may easily avoid debt collectors and court.

If you feel that you are being treated disrespectfully or rudely ask to be put through to a supervisor or manager. Don't get rude or angry, that doesn't help, you want them on your side. They are actually there to help. Years ago I was a consultant with Yes Car Credit and, in a conversation with one of the joint Managing Directors, he explained that, even though they were dealing with people that were some of the highest risk in the country, they would always look for ways to get the debt paid rather than collect the car. As he pointed out, collecting cars back doesn't earn them money, collecting payments does, even if they have to reduce the payments for a while.

Never threaten those that you owe money to or say that they must accept the payment offered or you will go bankrupt, that may get them motivated to take action before you get the chance to file for bankruptcy.

Mortgage Rescue Scheme

I don't want to go into detail about this, as few people extend their mortgage or take out a secured personal loan resulting in a second charge on their property for a car. However, if you have, there is a little bit of relief since the government introduced its 'mortgage rescue scheme' in autumn 2008. The guidance for the courts ensures that lenders take all reasonable steps to avoid repossession.

However, statistics have shown that few families have benefitted and, whilst major mortgage lenders have signed into the scheme, many smaller and second charge (secured loan) lenders haven't, resulting in houses being repossessed. You can get a great deal of advice from Citizen's Advice Bureau, Shelter, Money Advice Trust and Advice UK. If you end up in court and you are paying the mortgage holder and have suggested a payment plan to the second charge holder, the judge is very unlikely to grant a repossession order but he may do, so try your hardest to avoid court.

30 Day Rule

The government introduced a new rule on 6th April 2009 to allow those struggling to pay debts some breathing space. Borrowers will have 30 days after appointing an accredited debt adviser to take control of their finances. Under the agreement, debt collection agencies will not contact debtors to pursue debts for 30 days once they have been advised that an accredited debt advisor has taken on the case. This will allow the adviser to negotiate with the creditors and the debt collection agency so that a repayment plan can be agreed.

Accredited debt advisers include:

- Citizens Advice Bureaux
- Advice UK
- The Consumer Credit Counselling Service

The purpose is to relieve the pressure on those in debt and encourage those with problems to seek professional help. It also removes you from the negotiations, so it helps your peace of mind and the lenders seem happier to accept the same proposals made by an advisor than if they were made by you. If you explain to the advisor how important your car is for your work, family etc. he can construct a case to try to ensure that you keep your car.

Debt Relief Order/Bankruptcy

They both amount to the same: if you have insufficient assets to sell in order to satisfy your debts, you can go into bankruptcy or arrange a debt relief order (also known as the poor man's bankruptcy). The scope of this book does not allow me to go into detail but both are to be avoided if you can as they affect your ability to arrange credit in the future.

You are discharged from the Debt Relief Order/bankruptcy after 12 months, at the end of which you will be free of all debt shown on the order. However, it remains on your credit file for 6 years, during which time you are unlikely to be able to arrange credit. The cost of raising the order is £90 and this can be spread over 6 months. Bankruptcy costs £475 up front. You cannot arrange for a Debt Relief Order if you have:

- Things of value or savings over £300
- A vehicle worth more than £1,000
- Private pension fund worth over £300

An adviser can give you guidance over your eligibility and advise on other options that may be preferable. There are many constraints so you would really need to be caught in the poverty trap before you become eligible.

Guarantees/Indemnities

In order to secure a loan or car finance, a guarantee or indemnity may have been asked for by the lender. You may be acting as guarantor for a family member or you may be the person who has taken out the loan and now has to tell the guarantor that you haven't been able to make your payments. So what started out as a little bit of casual help now turns out to be a disaster. But all may not be lost, let me explain the procedures.

Let's be clear, before a lender considers a guarantor he must be fairly certain that the borrower can repay his debts. You may be someone who has never had credit before or you have had a credit card that has hardly been used, so you have very little credit history on which to form an opinion. But everything about you looks good, home, job, bank, etc., and you certainly have no adverse information stored on your credit file but, for extra comfort, the lender may be happy to accept a guarantor in order to agree the finance.

The hope is that the guarantor will never be called upon but in the current climate more and more individuals and businesses are failing or struggling, so it isn't surprising that fewer lessors are accepting guarantees. They would rather the customer was rock solid in the first place, especially as the lenders appear to have less money to lend than they have applicants.

The bad news is that when people have failed to make their payments, where a guarantor is involved, the finance company approaches them to make good the missed payments, which could run into thousands of pounds. If the guarantor is unable or unwilling to make the payments, he could also find himself in court and with adverse information stored against him on the credit files, making it difficult for him to arrange credit in the future in his own name - so beware.

However, this snippet of information could save you from all of this if you have signed a guarantee. You could, avoid making any payments and leave your credit unaffected. You can also use this to help the guarantor if you are the borrower. Much of what I'm about to talk about is in the wording of the guarantee/indemnity. First of all, what is the difference between a guarantee and an indemnity?

A guarantee is your promise to answer for the debt of another who still remains the one who is primarily liable for the debt. The liability of the guarantor is, in fact, secondary. On the other hand, if you provide an indemnity, it means that you, known as the surety, share primary responsibility with the borrower. In other words it is a little like being jointly and severally liable for a debt, eg. a mortgage in joint names. Now this is where it can get interesting.

Let's say you have signed up as a guarantor on a debt taken on by a friend or relation. The borrower has fallen behind with repayments and the lender has tried to collect the money without success making you now liable for the debt. In a final effort to recover money from the borrower, the lender agrees a payment schedule, i.e. reduced payments for 3 months then increased payments to bring the debt back into line. This then changes the responsibility of a guarantor if the borrower fails to make the revised payments.

This is not the agreement that you agreed to guarantee so, unless there was a term in the guarantee that allowed for a variation or time to pay without discharging the surety, you are no longer a guarantor. If you signed an indemnity then you are considered to be jointly liable and as responsible for the debt as the primary borrower. In summary, in the absence of an express term to the contrary in the guarantee, any bilateral variation of the contract between the creditor and the debtor, i.e. by allowing more time to pay, will discharge the liability of the guarantor. This is not the case with an indemnity where the liability of the surety, being a primary liability, survives.

This position was highlighted in the case of Associated British Ports v Ferryways NV and MSC Belgium NV, whereby MSC guaranteed the contractual obligations to Associated British Ports. When Ferryways were given more time to pay, following a dispute, the courts ruled (and confirmed on appeal) that this variation discharged the obligations of the guarantor. Had the guarantee provided that any subsequent variation or time to pay agreement between the claimant and Ferryways would not discharge the surety, the result would have been different. So, check the wording of a guarantee before you sign it and know your obligations.

What To Do When Things Go Wrong Part 2

In this section I will deal with specific problems that relate to individual finance methods. Whilst the need to communicate and the other items mentioned above apply to all types of finance, each different method has its own set of legal implications and each lender has a few impositions of his own contained within the terms and conditions of the contract. You remember the documents you signed, probably without reading them, when you arranged finance on your car – suddenly you will be wishing you had read and understood them. However, the good news is that lenders cannot contract you out of statutory terms and conditions so, whilst they may include a term that allows them to collect your car if you haven't kept up your payments in their contract, under the terms of the Consumer Credit Act, they may only be able to do this if they have previously obtained a court order. So fear not, my guide should help you through the situation.

Personal Loan - Secured

As mentioned above this is a dangerous type of finance as you can lose your house. The lenders warn you when you take out your loan that your home is at risk if you secure a loan against it. You need to do as suggested above, make contact with the lender and negotiate a payment schedule as soon as things go wrong. The lender cannot take your car but he can apply for a repossession order forcing you out of your house, selling it and recovering the money that you owe him, together with any 'reasonable' costs out of the sale proceeds. The truth is that repossession is not easy to obtain, especially if the amount owed is relatively small and the result would be a family that would need to be re-housed. But it is possible and it is well known that holders of second charges will push for repossession of the property more vigorously than first charge holders.

Many people are under the mistaken impression that as long as the repayments on their mortgage are kept up to date, their property is not at risk from being repossessed, following missed payments on a second charge loan. This is not the case. A second charge lender will pursue court action and ultimate possession of the property, subject to the court order being granted. In the event that the property is repossessed, and subsequently sold, the proceeds from the sale will firstly be used to pay off the outstanding first mortgage and then the balance of any further charges, in order of registration at the land registry. Any surplus funds will pass to the borrower.

It makes sense to do everything you can to repay the debt, or come to an arrangement with the lender, as you are no longer guaranteed to remain in your home if you keep your mortgage payments up to date but fall behind with repayments on a loan secured upon it. Always take advice from your financial advisor.

Personal Loan - Unsecured

As I have mentioned before, this is probably one of the most misunderstood finance products that people use to finance a car. However, it is also likely to be the cheapest so it proves to be very popular, especially as the perception is that the borrower will not lose anything if he defaults on the payments. This is simply not true, added to which your legal rights are pretty weak compared to say HP or a PCP.

Similar rules apply to an unsecured personal loan as they do to a secured personal loan when things go wrong. Your car cannot automatically be recovered if you default on your payments as the loan isn't secured against it. But you need to take action immediately if you are to manage to hold on to your car as well as other precious possessions.

That's right, everything you own (regarded as non essential) is at risk so don't think for one second that an unsecured loan will simply go away if you stop paying. If you are struggling to make the repayments on your loan, get in touch with the lender and see if you can be given a holiday period, whereby you make no payments for say 3 months, in order to give you time to arrange a new job, or maybe you have had a temporary drop in income due to illness, a new baby or, during the recession, an agreement with your employer to take a drop in income.

If this can't be agreed see what can be arranged by way of a reduced payment, always remember that a lender would rather collect money than your possessions, it is not good for publicity and causes a lot of aggravation and cost. When agreeing a temporary payment don't overstretch yourself, make sure you have worked out your income and expenditure before you contact the lender, that way you'll know exactly how much you can afford to pay and, of course, use one of the debt counselling agencies if it is all too much for you to deal with yourself – you are not alone.

If you are one of those who feels you can bury your head in the sand in the hope that the debt will simply go away, you should be aware that if you don't make contact the lender will have no choice but to pass the debt over to a debt collection agency. Even though new guidelines have been issued regarding debt collection, it is their job to collect outstanding debts so they are bound to be more aggressive in their approach than the lender.

However, they also want to collect money rather than goods so they are normally able to negotiate an arrangement on behalf of the lender. You should do it, try to keep your car if you consider it to be an essential. By now of course your credit file will show some adverse information. Had you made an arrangement with the lender before you went into arrears, you may well have avoided any adverse information being shown on your credit file.

If you still don't pay you will be taken to court. It is wise for you to attend and if the hearing is close to the lender's offices, as it normally is, and the distance is inconvenient or difficult for you to get to, you can apply to have the case moved to your local county court. You will be invited to provide a defence and required to provide an income and expenditure account. In your defence you will have the opportunity to explain why you are experiencing problems, no need to go into minute detail, just an overview of your circumstances.

Provide a clear breakdown of income and expenditure, again you can get help from a debt counselling agency as well as the court. They are actually very nice people and very helpful so don't be frightened to ask their advice. If you are in court the judge is far more likely to try his hardest to help you than if you are not, so please make an attempt to go, it really isn't as frightening as it might seem.

If you are frightened about a court appearance please don't be. Judges are there to help you and try to find a way for you to get out of debt as painlessly as possible. I am a very confident person but when I first went to court, following the collapse of my business, I was petrified but, you know what, it was quite painless. You are simply in a room with the judge and a solicitor from the lender.

The judge explains what is happening and confirms details of the debt with the solicitor. He then reads through your defence and your income and expenditure account. After several questions about your income and your ability to repay the debt he will talk to the solicitor and normally propose a payment schedule based on his conclusions after speaking to you.

He will now make a formal judgement – known as a Count Court Judgement (CCJ). This isn't great news as far as your credit rating is concerned, as a CCJ makes things worse and it stays on your file for six years, even after the judgement debt is repaid. You see how important it is to discuss the debt with the lender as soon as you know you are about to experience some difficulties.

Finally, if you don't make the payments as set out in the judgement, the debt collection agency will be back in court and, unless you have had a change in circumstances, an 'enforcement order' will be issued and a bailiff appointed to recover possessions from you to the value of the debt. If the bailiff feels that you don't have possessions sufficient to cover the debt and you own your home they can apply for a 'charging order'. If granted, the 'charge' is registered against your property and paid out of the proceeds of sale. Some creditors are happy to wait till you sell your property in order to recover the debt whilst others will immediately apply for an 'Order For Sale.' If this is likely to happen you need to take immediate advice in order to put a case to the court in order to prevent the order being granted.

A word of warning about charging orders, they are enforceable indefinitely. Unlike other debts that may be secured upon a property which can be time barred, this debt is still due even if the lender hasn't been in contact during the preceding years, so consider the consequences of a charging order if applied. It could affect your ability to move or your children's inheritance.

So you see, an unsecured loan isn't as it appears, it can actually be secured against all of your possessions, even your house. As I say in my presentations, an unsecured loan simply means the loan isn't secured against anything - in particular.

Hire Purchase/Personal Contract Purchase (PCP)

I am a big fan of HP and PCP when compared to personal loans because of the legal strength they provide to consumers. The transaction has to be covered by the Consumer Credit Act to fully benefit from all the legal rights attached to HP and PCP but, provided it is, you receive a great deal of legal cover when things go wrong. And I'm not just talking about when things go wrong financially, you also have greater protection if you have problems with your car. Under section 75 of the Consumer Credit Act if you feel you have been miss-sold the car or it has been misrepresented, you can sue not only the supplying dealer but also the lender, something you can't do if you pay cash or use a loan.

What few people are aware of is their position if they paid cash to a dealer for a car but paid a small deposit by credit card. Should the car have been misrepresented or there has been a breach of contract you are still able to sue either the dealer or the credit card company or both and, as the Financial Ombudsman Service points out, "The claim is not limited to the amount of the credit card transaction. Customers can claim for all losses caused by the breach of contract or misrepresentation. And this applies even if all they paid by credit card was the deposit." Some great advice there for anyone wanting at least part of the protection of the Consumer Credit Act but still pay cash. By paying just £10 on your credit card you are covered on a purchase up to £30,000.

You should also be aware that if you have an HP or PCP agreement, under section 75 of the Consumer Credit Act you can sue the dealer, the finance company or both if you have been miss-sold, the car has been misrepresented or there has been a breach of contract. Some lenders have told customers that they must first obtain a court judgement against the supplier (dealer) before they can involve the finance company – this isn't true. Who to sue is your choice. In fact the Financial Ombudsman Service has awarded compensation to consumers who have been misled, and claims delayed, by the lenders making false claims about their responsibility.

On your PCP or HP agreement you will see two key figures shown under **Repossession – Your Rights and Termination - Your Rights**. Dealing with repossession: you can have your car repossessed if you fail to make payments to the lender at any time until you have paid a third of the total amount payable. The lender doesn't need a court order to repossess your car, provided the car is parked in a public area. If the car is parked in a private area he will need a court order to repossess the goods, as he would do if you have paid over a third of the total amount owed. If they collect the car and do not comply with the legal obligations, you are entitled to a refund of all money paid to the lender.

Before any action can take place, the lender has to give you at least 7 days to bring your payments up to date and have issued you with a default notice in writing. You are not legally obliged to respond to any contact made by the lender other than in writing. As emphasised above you should contact the lender as soon as you know you are going to run into difficulties and negotiate a plan before things go tragically wrong. There are ways to keep your car.

Once a court order has been issued, you can apply to the court for a time order to be applied. You can do this on form Time Order Form, N440, which can be obtained from the court or downloaded from the internet. This will normally be granted if you are experiencing a temporary setback, eg. recovering from an accident/operation and receiving sick benefit or maybe redundancy with a view to getting another job, especially if you are dependent on the car for your work.

Another great legal right that you have is the ability to terminate your agreement once you have paid 50% of the total amount owed, shown on your contract as **Termination – Your Rights**. I was asked by Paul Lewis on Radio 4's Money Box programme why anyone would want to hand a car back once they have paid 50% of the debt. The answer was simple, because at that point the car is normally in negative equity and, as this is a legal entitlement, you can happily pass the loss over to the lender by exercising your right to Voluntarily Terminate (VT) the agreement. Technically this is known as sections 99 and 100 of the Consumer Credit Act.

This can save you thousands of pounds, as one of my customers found out when he VT'd his Volvo. When he asked for a settlement cost from the HP company he was given a figure that was £4,000 more than he could raise for the car in a part exchange. As he had paid back over 50% of the amount owed on the agreement he simply handed the car back and saved himself the £4,000. Some people VT their car to avoid a loss but others do it because it is a necessity, i.e., they can no longer afford to make payments or, as happened to one customer, she could no longer drive the car following an accident that damaged her back.

As a note goes on to your credit file to say that you have VT'd the car, it may affect your ability to obtain finance in the future, especially if you have done it several times. However, if you have special circumstances it would be wise to tell future lenders by posting a Notice Of Correction on all of your credit files. More of this later. That is a great tip –

another is to make sure that you put your request to VT the car in writing. An insider in one of the top three credit reference agencies told me that it is quite common for people who have VT'd their car to have a default registered against them because they didn't stick to the procedures shown in their agreement by putting the VT in writing. Once a default has been registered in these circumstances there is virtually nothing you can do to have the default removed. Try taking out finance with a default registered against you?

Contract Hire & Personal Contract Hire (PCH)

As you never own the car under a contract hire agreement, the position is somewhat more straight-forward. The contract hire company or lessor can provide you with a simple settlement figure, which you have to pay to hand the car back. Or you can agree a figure with the lender, which includes the cost of the car, so by paying this amount you get to keep the car.

However, this figure will include a settlement charge. Some people think that, as you don't own the vehicle, you can just hand the car back as you can with a daily rental vehicle. This isn't true, you enter into a fixed term agreement and you are, therefore, expected to keep the car for this period. Having said this, the lender is not allowed to charge a penalty in English law. He can recover his costs –

but how can you prove if you are being charged a penalty within the early termination fee?

Well, one precaution would be to arrange quotes based on 2 years as well as 3 years, in the event that you take out a 3 year agreement but terminate after 2 years. This has to be done when you take out your 3 year agreement It then becomes a simple exercise to calculate how much you would have paid over 2 years had you taken out a 2 year contract compared to what you have actually paid. You will probably find that you should be paying much less than the invoiced settlement figure.

As a rule of thumb, contract hire companies will charge 50% of outstanding rentals, although some have been charging up to 95% of outstanding rentals, which should be challenged by writing to the Office of Fair Trading and the Financial Ombudsman Service. If the lender is found to be charging a penalty, the whole contract could be set aside leaving you with no settlement fee to pay.

There is a landmark case which you can refer to when you make your formal complaint to the Financial Ombudsman Service. The case is Volkswagen Financial Services vs George Ramage 2007. Mr Ramage fell into arrears following which VW tried to charge all outstanding rentals. The Court of Appeal ruled that as no account had been taken of the higher value of the car that the charge for all outstanding rentals was in part a penalty and therefore unenforceable.

As with other forms of finance, the most important thing for you to do is contact the lender and explain if you are having problems. If you are having a short term problem then you may be able to negotiate a holiday period whereby you pay nothing for 3 months or maybe a reduced payment for three months.

If you see no way through, then you should make sure that you hand the car back to the lender, rather than wait to have it repossessed which will add to the charges. The courts will go easier on you if you do your best to mitigate the loss that the lender will experience.

There are a number of contract hire companies that offer a lease takeover but this is very dangerous. If you have someone that would like to take over your payments then you should tell the lender. They will need to carry out a credit search on the person or company that is willing to take over the repayments before agreeing and issuing an assignment. But be very careful. If you have a property on lease and someone agrees to take over the lease but they fail to make payments you are still liable.

The same applies to some cars. The lender agrees to the assignment but if the new customer doesn't pay the lease you could still be liable. If this is the case, challenge it. Even worse are some of these specialist takeover companies that say they will arrange for a lease takeover. They normally have clients that would not get approved on finance but would like to take over your repayments. But you have to remember that these people are poor credit risks and would probably not be able to lease a car in their own names. The arrangement is for the new lessee to take the car and sign a direct debit to pay the monthly rental into your account.

However, if they stop repayments, you are still liable to make the payments, even though you don't have the car. The police are loathe to get involved as you voluntarily handed over the keys and you will find that if the car is damaged or involved in an accident you are liable as the car should be insured by you. You will find that the original contract has a 'no sub-let' clause which means you can only offset the lease with the approval of the leasing company.

Don't forget that you will be invoiced for any excess mileage charges on a pro-rata basis along with any necessary body or interior repairs to damage caused by the person who took over your lease. Once you know the charges and have challenged them, as mentioned above, and agreed a final figure with the funder, you can then make an offer to repay the agreed amount over a period if you need time to pay. That way you avoid additional costs although it will be too late to help your credit status.

Notice Of Correction

A Notice Of Correction is a note of 200 words maximum that can be added to your file held by any credit reference agency; I have mentioned it several times in this book. The notice enables you to bring to the attention of anyone checking your file any contributory factors that led to an adverse situation, such as missed credit card payments or arrears and CCJ's.

You can mention that you were made redundant or suffered some illness and explain what you have done to correct the situation. You mustn't say anything derogatory about the ex that dumped you for her boss leaving you with all the debt, or the company that was so badly managed it made you redundant after 20 years of loyal service, but when you leave a message the underwriter <u>must</u> read it if you have applied for credit, although they are not obliged to take it into account. Keep it clear, concise and believable.

Don't forget to register the same note with all 3 major credit reference agencies as different lenders use different credit reference agencies. Don't forget to remove the notice if the adverse information, such as arrears or defaults, are removed from your file. It would be a cause for concern if you have a notice referring to some arrears that have subsequently been removed.

The safest way to register a Notice of Correction would be to write to the credit reference agencies individually and send your letter by recorded delivery. You may be able to log onto the websites and record the notices individually via their websites, but they seem to change their websites every 5 minutes so it may be better to simply write. Don't bother phoning as you will end up in a telephone cascade pressing numerous buttons, getting nowhere and end up throwing something at the cat! Addresses of the credit reference agencies are at the back of this book.

Conclusion

I hope you have found the above interesting and of use. I can't stress enough the importance of preparing for finance. Contrary to common belief, the lenders are very limited by the amount of money they have available to lend, with some only having enough money to lend to the top 20% of applicants. If this is the case, a little bit of care taken before you make an application could save a lot of grief and generate a few extra points on your credit score that could make the difference between acceptance and decline, or low prime lending rates compared to high, sub prime lending rates. It's all down to preparation.

Choosing the most suitable finance isn't easy given the fact that there are over 40 ways to finance a car and the car finance industry is poorly regulated, leaving the door open to every crook and charlatan to rip you off without fear. The problem with the law in this sector is that it is 'after the fact'. There are remedies if you find that you have been ripped off but nothing in place to prevent being ripped off in the first place. So follow my advice, keep your wits about you and if you are worried about car finance, use a professional broker like me who is a member of a trade or professional association such as the British Vehicle Rental and Leasing Association (BVRLA) or the National Association of Commercial Finance Brokers (NACFB).

Finally, none of us expects the worst to happen but it's a sad fact of life that it can and does. An accident, death of a close one, loss of a 'secure' job, terrorist attack, unexpected hurricanes, these can all contribute to a personal financial crisis. If this happens we need to know how to best deal with it, so I hope that my notes will help you to deal with the problems and recover from it as quickly and as painlessly as possible. As I have said already, I have experienced the problems first hand so I know what I'm talking about. The good news is that there are many specialists available to you, free of charge to help to take the pressure off at a time when you are least able to deal with debt problems.

More help and advice will continue to be posted weekly on my blog by going to:

www.thebestcarfinanceblog.co.uk

Good luck and best wishes, don't forget to let me know through my blog if the book helped.

Addendum: The Effects Of The EU Consumer Credit Act

I have seen many changes in finance regulations over the years but never have I experienced such a dog's dinner as that imposed by the EU by way of the EU Consumer Credit Directive. Every member state has its own set of rules, when it comes to the regulation of consumer finance, so it's impossible to apply a standard set of rules to every country without changing the very core of their finance systems that have built up over decades.

For example most countries have a form of Conditional Sale Agreement, something we have in the UK but we use a more popular, but similar, product called Hire Purchase. However, because it doesn't fit the 'standard model' for Conditional Sale it has been excluded from the directive. But if the Hire Purchase rules remained the same it would throw the UK into chaos so we have had to change the rules governing HP within the Consumer Credit Act to bring the rules into line with the directive governing Conditional Sale Agreements, ruled upon by the Directive. Clear? As mud probably! But as the changes affect us all it is important that you are aware of the changes and their affects. More important to us all are the products that remain outside the regulations and remain potentially open to abuse.

I was trying to work out an analogy when explaining the EU Consumer Credit Directive and I came up with 'It's a little like the EU deciding that it would apply standard driving regulations across every country in Europe neglecting to allow for the small, but significant fact, that we drive on the correct side of the road whilst the rest of Europe drives on the right. So if one of the rules was – when approaching a roundabout, check for traffic approaching from the left we would end up with some amazing crashes across the whole of the roundabout capital, Milton Keynes, along with the rest of the country.' But to complicate things further it's a little like saying that the new driving rules only apply to cars and commercials but ignore motorcyclists. Who said that they take no notice anyway? You see what I mean, for harmonisation you would have to change the core and work out otherwise we end up with what we have – a complete bodge job!

OK I'm going to try to summarise the main changes as they affect you bearing in mind that this was all aimed to make life easier for the consumer. Bear in mind also that I have yet to find two lenders who have put exactly the same interpretation on all the changes.

Who's Affected?

In the UK we have regulations that treat small businesses as consumers, however, the new regulations do not recognise small businesses as consumers so the regulations, as applied to businesses remain pretty much unchanged, except where the Department for Business Innovation & Skills (BIS) has decided it is pertinent to bring both sectors into line with the new ruling. Yep as I said – a bloody dog's dinner!

I should explain before going any further that the EU Consumer Credit Directive isn't law in this country. We set our own laws, the main one affecting consumer credit is the Consumer Credit Act. As a result of the directive we have carried out some amendments to these existing regulations and added a few sections in order to implement the rules. Just so that we are crystal clear – we just do as we're told.

Key Changes

These are changes required by the CCD on existing rules within the UK's Consumer Credit Act (CCA).

Early Repayment

You may have seen on finance agreements your right to pay off the loan early. This was covered by

Section 94 of the CCA. The same basis for calculating the settlement figure when fully repaying a loan is now being used to enable consumers to <u>partially</u> repay their loans but with a new formula. You will be informed (if you ask the lender) as to how the repayment affects future payments along with the outstanding balance. Where a fixed rate loan is settled early and the amount exceeds £8,000 over a 12 month period the lender can claim compensation of up to 1% of the early repayment figure. This is now section 95a of the CCA which also states that the compensation figure must be both fair and objectively justified. Here we go, how do you decide that other than in a court? Why bother saying anything – bloody daft!

Contractual Information

The new regulations set out the information that must be provided to consumers entering into credit agreements. This is somewhat different to the information that was required previously and must be shown in a way that is 'clear and concise', whatever that means, another court case pending I think. Where agreements fall outside the scope of the CCD, lenders can however continue to rely upon previous legislation.

APR Calculation

A new standard method of calculation has been introduced although, according to BIS, there will be no significant change to the resultant figures. In my opinion, and this is just my opinion, APR is the most ridiculous figure ever created. It is a dangerous standard, confuses the true cost of finance and should never be used as a means of comparison between finance products. It is only a meaningful figure if you are a mathematician, as a consumer it is a rubbish way of drawing a conclusion as to which product to select! If you want to compare products just compare the cost of credit for each. Or more important ask yourself one simple question – CAN I AFFORD IT?

Variation of Interest Rates

BIS has changed the way that consumers must be notified about any changes in interest rates, not just those within the CCD. When interest rates are changed, when they are not linked to a reference rate, this must be notified in advance. On the other hand when changes to interest rates are implemented, when linked to a reference rate, the lender no longer needs to notify the consumer purely due to the changes being advertised in branches or newspapers. Instead the consumers need to be advised personally, periodically and in durable form.

Credit Intermediaries

Intermediaries who provide their own documentation now have to declare their status to consumer customers in their advertising and in other materials. They must explain whether they are independent or working exclusively with one or more lenders (new section 54B). They must also disclose any fees chargeable to the customer in writing (new section 54C) and then pass this information to the lender who should then factor this information into the APR (new section 54D). Where the commission is paid by the lender there seems to be no such provision to declare the amount charged although there seems to be a common law requirement on the intermediary to explain that he will receive a commission without having to declare the amount. It is a moot point as to the extent that this applies to HP agreements – back to court!

Exemptions

Previously all agreements that fell within the scope of the CCA were covered by it. However, where a loan is to be repaid within 12 months, there is no interest to pay and there are limited payments (less than four) this agreement would qualify for exemption. Can't see too many agreements falling into that category.

A previous exemption was the 'high net worth' exemption, i.e. it allowed very wealthy individuals to opt out of regulation, whatever the value of the transaction. This has now been amended to only apply to loans above £60,260 but then as you will see later loans above this figure are out of the scope of the CCD anyway. Confused? Transactions below this figure will now fall within the scope of the CCA.

New Requirements

The above covered areas that already existed within the CCA but were amended as a result of the EU CCD. The following items cover the new requirements that have had to be included into the UK's Consumer Credit Act (CCA).

Adequate Explanations

This is new section 55A of the Consumer Credit Act (CCA) created out of articles 4,5 and 6 of the CCD. Here we go again, court cases looming here I think for those trying to extract themselves from finance agreements.

There must be adequate explanations of matters such as the cost of credit, any features of the agreement that may have an unforeseen significant adverse effect on the consumer, the consequences of not making payments on time (including legal proceedings), the existence of right of withdrawal and how to ask for further explanations or information.

The adequate explanation should enable the consumer to decide if the loan suits their needs and circumstances (but unless they know all the options available how will they know?). It must also be 'in good time' before the consumer is bound by the agreement. This information must be in the form of the Pre-Contract Credit Information also known as the Standard European Consumer Credit Information (SECCI). In the case of overdrafts this is known as the European Consumer Credit Information form. This is not dissimilar in concept to the previous pre-contract information although the new form is highly prescriptive and different in nature. Information required is set out in the Consumer Credit (Disclosure of Information) regulations 2010. The explanations need not be provided by the lender if the explanations have been provided by a credit intermediary (previously known as a credit broker). Adequate explanations do not apply to loans provided to consumers for loans above EUR 75,000 (£60,260).

For me the whole thing revolves around the wording 'adequate explanations'. This is a 'fixall' for every consumer which can't work. An adequate explanation to an Accountant or Financial Advisor will not be an adequate explanation to someone who doesn't know the meaning of the word 'interest'. It is so ridiculous and has the potential to cause dealers, brokers and lenders all sorts of legal problems. Make sure that you fully understand all aspects of the finance and if you are unsure ask.

Requirement to Assess Credit Worthiness

It is not believed that lenders will dramatically change their underwriting process and credit scoring the new regulations, section 55B, state that they are now required to assess a consumer's credit worthiness on the basis of 'sufficient information' before concluding a credit agreement. The information is to be obtained from the debtor, where appropriate, and a credit reference agency where this is necessary. Here we go again! Guidance has been provided by the Office of Fair Trading (OFT) which can be found on their web site under the heading 'Irresponsible Lending – OFT Guidance for Creditors'

Requirement Concerning Credit Reference Databases

This is article 9 of the CCD. Lenders do not have to consult a Credit Reference Agency before making a decision to lend. However, if they do and end up rejecting the application they are obliged to provide to the applicant the search results and full details of the credit reference agency database consulted. This must be done immediately and at no charge. This change to the CCA section 157 would result in charges against the lender if he doesn't comply as it is regarded as a criminal offence.

Right of Withdrawal

This is covered in the new section 74A of the CCA. Previously you could withdraw from an agreement up to 5 days after execution of an agreement (execution is when both the lender and customer have signed). This has been replaced with a right to withdraw up to 14 days after a contract has been concluded, or from the day after the customer has received the contractual Terms and Conditions if later. The lender must receive a notification to withdraw by the customer, either by phone or in writing, effective on the date of posting. The lender can specify someone else to receive the notification on his behalf. This also replaces the 'on trade premises' rule which meant that if an agreement was signed on trade premises the customer had no right of withdrawal. The new rules also cover hire purchase agreements, pawn broking agreements and business loans below £25,000. The right will not apply to consumer loans above £60,260. The customer must repay the capital and interest accrued between drawdown and repayment.

Voluntary Termination

This was originally set up to allow customers in severe financial difficulty to extract themselves painlessly from Hire Purchase agreements. When they had paid 50% of the total amount owed plus arrears they could simply hand the goods back to the lender. However this happened in the days when most people put down a 25% or 30% deposit and when the car was handed back, after paying the 50%, it was worth more or about the same as the settlement figure.

These days the VT provision is abused and should be replaced by something that actually helps those in trouble rather than give people the means to remove themselves from an agreement simply because they fancy a change or a dealer has encouraged them to do so in order to sell them another car. Whilst many expected the VT rule to be repealed the BIS has chosen not to change them. The argument for change comes from the idea that the purpose of the CCD was complete harmonisation across Europe without member states being able to provide greater benefits than others. However, as the CCD does not cover the area of Voluntary Termination, the BIS has chosen to leave it in the current legislation. The CCD only covers early settlement and right of withdrawal at the beginning of the agreement.

The BIS stated that 'The Government does not believe that the VT provisions are incompatible with rights to settle early and rights of withdrawal within the CCD. Early repayment is about early performance of the contract rather than termination, while the exercise of the right of withdrawal can be most correctly described as cancellation of the agreement'. Thus they believe that termination is not affected by the CCD so can stand. It looks as though the only way this will be settled is through a court challenge by a creditor.

Assignment of Rights

A notice of assignment must be given to a customer if arrangements for administration of their agreement are assigned such that the rights of the customer are affected. Doesn't really mean much unless, for example, the method of collecting payments change.

'Out of Scope' Agreements

Certain types of agreement fall within the Consumer Credit Act but fall outside the CCD, these are known as 'Out of Scope' Agreements. For the sake of clarity I have shown them below:

- Lending to small businesses, partnerships and unincorporated bodies

- Loans below EUR 200 (this has been set at £160)

- Loans above EUR 75,000 (this has been set at £60,260)

- Second charge mortgages

- Hire Purchase agreements (although as its sister product, conditional sale is included the CCA has been adjusted to bring both products in line)

- Credit with no interest or other significant charges and repayable within 3 months.

- Consumer Hire Agreements

Here's where it all gets very strange because it would seem that when a contract is out of scope it can simply fall back on existing legislation. However the BIS has said that if lenders want to conform to the new legislation they can if they want – how daft is that?

Business Lending

The CCD excludes business lending but the BIS intends to apply the amending provisions of the CCD to business lending included in the CCA (ie. business lending up to £25,000). However the following CCD requirements will not apply to business lending:

- Advertising requirements (Article 4 CCD)

- Mandatory use of the SECCI although pre-contract information will have to be provided

- Mandatory compliance with CCD contractual information requirements, although contractual information will still have to be provided.

- The requirement to provide amortisation tables, ie. a table detailing periodic payment of interest and the principal balance of a loan, on demand

Loans Above £60,260

Again the BIS proposes that loans covered by the CCA that are above the CCD threshold of £60,260 should be subject to the CCD's requirements. However the following provisions of the CCD will not apply to such loans:

- Mandatory use of the SECCI although pre-contract information will have to be provided

- Mandatory compliance with CCD contractual information requirements, although contractual information will still have to be provided.

- The right of withdrawal

- The requirement to provide amortisation tables, i.e. a table detailing periodic payment of interest and the principal balance of a loan, on demand

- The requirement to provide adequate explanations.

Advertisements

There are a number of changes that have been introduced that all adverts must conform to. The most important change relates to APR. When APR is shown on an advertisement for consumers the APR must be designated 'Representative APR' and it must relate to at least 51% of all agreements issued. As opposed to what we had before which was 66%. Can't quite work out how that benefits consumers, they stand to be worse off now because the 49% can be charged anything but the lender can still advertise the rate that will only be provided to 51% of the borrowers. Bloody crazy.

Addendum

There are numerous new requirements included in the Consumer Credit (Advertisements) Regulations 2010, too many to mention. If you are an advertiser you should take legal advice before placing an ad.

Conclusion

As mentioned before the whole thing is a dog's dinner. I have identified over 40 ways to finance a car and yet there is no obligation on the salesperson to explain all of the options available to a customer, or even some of them. There are contradictions and loose ends with some of the new rules applying to small businesses whilst others don't and what will happen when a lender decides to drop VT off their HP agreement? Customers will be in a complete mess. As a result of the change to advertising consumers may well end up paying over the odds for a loan believing they will be offered the loan at the advertised rate when they end up being charged substantially more. The one area that needs some very serious controls introduced is the area of leasing. It is much more complicated and the source of much confusion and fraudulent activities. The above views expressed are purely personal. I would also add that if you wanted to enter into a finance agreement you should consult your solicitor if you are confused about anything.

Sources: Various including Wragge & Co

Contacts & Resources

Office Of Fair Trading
Enquiries & Reporting Centre
Fleetbank House
2-6 Salisbury Square
London
EC4Y 8JX
Tel: 08454 04 05 06
Email: enquiries@oft.gsi.gov.uk
Web: www.consumerdirect.gov.uk/

Citizens Advice Bureau
Check Yellow Pages For Local Office or
Website: http://www.citizensadvice.org.uk/
Tel: 0844 848 9600

Consumer Direct
Tel: 08454 04 05 06
Email: Send email via website
Web: http://www.consumerdirect.gov.uk

Consumer Credit Counselling Service
Wade House
Merrion Centre
Leeds   LS2 8NG
Tel: 0800 138 1111
Email: contactus@cccs.co.uk
Web: http://www.cccs.co.uk

Financial Ombudsman Service
South Quay Plaza
183 Marsh Wall
London
E14 9SR
Tel: 0845 080 1800
Fax: 020 7964 1001
Email: complaint.info@financial-ombudsman.org.uk
Web: www.financial-ombudsman.org.uk

National Debtline
Tricorn House
51-53 Hagley Road
Edgbaston
Birmingham
B16 8TP
Tel: 0808 808 4000
Fax: 0121 410 6230
Email: Send email via website – contact us
Web: http://www.nationaldebtline.co.uk

Financial Services Authority (FSA)
25 The North Colonnade
Canary Wharf
London
E14 5HS
Tel: 0300 500 5000
Fax: 020 7066 1099
Email: Via Website – Follow Link:

http://www.moneymadeclear.fsa.gov.uk/contactus.aspx
Web: http://www.fsa.gov.uk

HPI Ltd
Dolphin House
New Street
Salisbury
Wiltshire
SP1 2PH
Tel: 01722 422 422
Fax: 01722 412 164
Email: Via Website – Follow Link:
http://www.raccheck.com/contact.html
Web: http://www.hpi.co.uk

National Association of Commercial Finance Brokers (NACFB)
3 Silverdown Office Park
Fair Oak Close
Exeter
Devon
EX5 2UX
Tel: 01392 440040
Email: admin@nacfb.org.uk
Web: http://www.nacfb.org

Finance & Leasing Association (FLA)
2nd Floor
Imperial House
15-19 Kingsway
London
WC2B 6UN
Tel: 020 7836 6511
Fax: 020 7420 9600
Email: info@fla.org.uk
Web: http://www.fla.org.uk

British Vehicle Rental and Leasing Association (BVRLA)
River Lodge
Badminton Court
Amersham
Bucks
HP7 0DD
Tel: 01494 434747
Fax: 01494 434499
Email: info@bvrla.co.uk
Web: http://www.bvrla.co.uk

Experian
Landmark House
Experian Way
NG2 Business Park
Nottingham
NG80 1ZZ
Tel: 0844 481 8000

Email: Via Web Site
Web: http://www.experian.co.uk

Callcredit Limited
One Park Lane
Leeds
West Yorkshire
LS3 1EP
Tel: 0113 244 1555
Fax: 0113 234 0050
Email Via Website -
http://www.callcredit.co.uk/contact.aspx
Web: http://www.callcredit.co.uk

Equifax Credit File Advice Centre
P.O. Box 1140
Bradford
BD1 5US
Tel: 0844 41 46 073
Email: Via Web Site
Web: www.equifax.co.uk

Printed in Great Britain
by Amazon